East Side Story

Ten Years with the
Jewish Repertory Theatre

Irene Backalenick

UNIVERSITY
PRESS OF
AMERICA

Lanham • New York • London

Copyright © **1988** by

University Press of America,® Inc.

4720 Boston Way
Lanham, MD 20706

3 Henrietta Street
London WC2E 8LU England

British Cataloging in Publication Information Available

Library of Congress Cataloging-in-Publication Data

Backalenick, Irene, 1921–
East side story.

Bibliography: p.
1. Jewish Repertory Theatre—History. 2. Jewish theater—New York (N.Y.)—
History—20th century.
PN3035.B28 1988   792'.09747'1   87–31633 CIP
ISBN 0–8191–6495–X (alk. paper)

Acknowledgements

This book was over two years in preparation, and many people helped along the way.

At the top of the list are two men who played key roles—Charles Gattnig and Ran Avni. Dr. Gattnig was my advisor at the City University of New York Graduate Center. I received my Doctor of Philosophy degree in theater history there in May 1987, and my doctoral dissertation formed the basis for this book. Dr. Gattnig guided me through the thickets of academic research with infinite patience and knowledge.

I also want to thank the other professors on my advisory committee, Dr. Vera Roberts and Dr. Margaret Knapp, for their suggestions and their careful reading of the manuscript.

Ran Avni, artistic director of the Jewish Repertory Theatre, gave me many, many hours of his time, as we explored the theater's history together. His recollections of the JRT's past and his impressions of the people involved are, of course, the very core of this book. We have preserved these many interviews on tape, and I believe they will enhance the JRT archives. I am also grateful for the many photographs culled from the JRT files. The theater was most generous in letting me use these historic materials.

I also want to thank Don Geller, executive director the Emanu-El Midtown YM-YWHA (home of the JRT), and Alfred Plant, chairman of the JRT board, for generously opening the theater's files to me and for offering their views and impressions.

I am especially grateful to Edward M. Cohen, associate director of the JRT, who drew me to this study in the first place because of his unwavering belief in the theater and his enthusiastic, articulate accounts of its accomplishments.

Many people connected with the JRT, too numerous to list individually, were generous with their time and their recollections—writers, directors, actors, set designers.

In another category entirely is Dan Edelman, my computer mentor. I could never have completed the onerous task of preparing this manuscript without his advice and active help.

Finally, I want to thank my husband William for his concrete help, humor, and tolerance as I worked with this all-absorbing, lengthy project.

Table of Contents

List of Tables

Introduction

*You cannot write a love story of two human beings without
dealing with their background. To whom did this person belong, and what language did his father speak at home, and so
on. Of course, we know that you are writing about a man. But
the question is: What man? Where does he come from? You
have to give his address.* [1]

Isaac Bashevis Singer's words capture the very essence of theater. If
theater is to reach audiences in the truest sense, it must be rooted in the
culture of its people.

This book examines one such theater in one particular time, a Jewish theater in contemporary America, a theater that seeks its sustenance
from the heritage of its people.

In this multi-ethnic country we have come to define theater that identifies with a particular heritage as ethnic theater, a term and an idea that has become fashionable of late. Indeed, the current climate is so hospitable that ethnic theaters of all persuasions are enjoying high visibility.

But the fact is that ethnic theater is as old as the history of any people. For the Jews, theater reaches far back in time, struggling to assert itself over the centuries, despite religious proscriptions. It reached a golden age in the nineteenth century with its Yiddish theater, which was, says Irving Howe,

> superbly alive and full of claptrap, close to the nerve of folk sentiment and outrageous in its pretensions to serious culture.[2]

Today's American Jewish theater is part of that centuries-old development. Though the current movement bears some resemblance to the Yiddish theater of the last century, and is frequently confused with it, it is, in fact, quite different. In order to explore similarities and differences, to examine the nature of Jewish theater today, I have focussed on one theater that personifies the new movement, the Jewish Repertory Theatre.

A problem immediately arises, resulting from semantics and ignorance. When one mentions Jewish theater, listeners invariably identify it as the old Yiddish theater, launching into tales of childhood visits to Second Avenue. But that theater flourished in an era now long gone and survives primarily in nostalgia and in memory. The term ''Yiddish theater'' refers to theater of a particular time and particular language. ''Jewish theater,'' on the other hand, refers to theater in any language and time that deals with the Jewish experience.

Today the new American Jewish theater is as relevant to the English-speaking Jews of the 1980s as the earlier Yiddish theater was to its time and people. The new wave theater differs in content, philosophy and, of course, language. Yiddish has been replaced by English. Melodrama and folklore have been replaced to a great extent by realism and contemporary political and sociological issues. The literature still deals with Jewish themes and the Jewish experience, but it aims at today's audiences.

With new professional companies springing up across the country, the movement is thriving—a renaissance and, yet, not quite a renaissance. It still represents a fledgling effort compared to the glory of Yiddish theatre at its zenith; most performing groups across the country have not achieved full professional status. However, and not surprisingly, New York City is leading the way, with three professional companies.

There are also professional companies in San Francicso, Berkeley, Miami, and Chicago. In addition, semi-professinal and non-professional groups exist in dozens of American cities and a few Canadian cities.

The Jewish Repertory Theatre, in the vanguard of the movement, can well serve as the movement's prototype. Again and again, the JRT has introduced plays—contemporary Jewish dramas as well as revivals and translations—that have been picked up later by other Jewish theaters.

In examining the movement, and the formative years of this particular theater, I posed the following questions: What exactly is Jewish theater as it exists in this country today? How does it differ from and what is its relationship to the Yiddish theater of the past? What are its goals? What kinds of plays does it present? What audiences does it attract?

In looking at the JRT's first ten years, 1975 to 1985, I directed my attention to its practical and philosophic concerns. How did the JRT manage to turn a dance classroom into a professional theater space? How did it upgrade its level of productions? How did it build a nucleus of playwrights, directors, actors, set designers, and technical help? How did it reach out and capture an audience? What was the source of its financial support? Above all, did it have a unique voice and how was that identity achieved?

In writing about this subject, one approaches virgin territory. Literature about the current genre, with the exception of occasional articles, simply does not exist. The bulk of my research has involved contact with primary sources, and I have depended upon old programs, theater reviews, office files, and personal interviews. Many hours were spent interviewing Ran Avni, founder and artistic director of the JRT. Other interviews have been conducted with actors, directors, playwrights, set designers, composers, JRT staff people, and Y officials. I have built a library of taped interviews that eventually will be turned over to the JRT for its archives.

Moreover, I have served, for the past several years, as New York theater critic for the *Jewish post and Opinion*, a group of Jewish newspapers published in Indianapolis. In the process I have had direct exposure to Jewish theater, having seen all the JRT productions, as well as many other dramas of Jewish interest.

Considerable background literature has helped me put the JRT history into a broader perspective. The most useful books for this purpose were: *How We Lived—A Documentary History of Immigrant Jews in America, 1880-1930,* by Irving Howe and Kenneth Libo, Richard March Publishers, 1979, New York; *Yiddish Theater in America,* by David Lifson, T. Yoseloff, 1965, New York; *Bright Star of Exile,* by Lulla Rosenfeld, Thomas Y. Crowell Company, 1977, New York; and (probably the most helpful book) Nahma Sandrow's *Vagabond Stars,* Harper & Row, 1977, New York.

Specifically helpful in terms of Jewish history were Irving Howe's *World of our Fathers,* Harcourt Brace Jovanovich, 1976, New York, and Oscar Handlin's book, *Adventure in Freedom, 300 Years of Jewish Life in America,* Kennikat Press, Port Washington, N.Y., 1971.

Plays of Jewish Interest, which was edited by Edward M. Cohen, associate director of the Jewish Repertory Theatre, and published by the Jewish Theater Association, New York, 1983, helped me to flesh out the image of the Jew in drama, as did *The Image of the Jew in American Literature* by Louis Harap, Jewish Publication Society of America, Philadelphia, 1978.

For a general background on ethnic theater, I referred to *Ethnic Theater in the United States,* edited by Maxine Seller, Greenwood Press, Westport, Connecticut, 1983.

My methodology has been to examine the JRT history chronologically, season by season, perusing programs, theater reviews, and feature articles on the productions, as well as interviewing people involved in various productions.

In order to reach the JRT theatergoers and to get their views about the company directly, a questionnaire was developed. The questionnaires were slipped into programs for the spring 1985 production of *Crossing Delancey.* People were asked to leave the completed forms in the lobby or return them by mail. The ten-percent return on the survey did indeed give a sense of the JRT theatergoers and their views.

While some of the dissertation's seven chapters are chronological, others are thematic. Specifically, the dissertation is organized as follows: Chapter 1 is a brief survey of Jewish attitudes toward theater over a 5000-year period of Jewish history. Chapter 2 covers the early years, both in Israel and the United States, of founder Ran Avni. Chapters 3 and 4 take the JRT through its first ten years, from its tentative beginnings to its significant later successes of *Kuni-Leml* and *Crossing Delancey*. Chapter 5 presents the young playwrights whose works have developed within the JRT's Playwrights-in-Residence program. Chapter 6 is also an in-depth study, a profile of the JRT theatergoers. Chapter 7 is the conclusion.

Since this is the first time a study has been made of the Jewish Repertory Theatre or, to my knowledge, of any phase of the current Jewish theater movement, I hope that this work will serve a useful purpose. I submit it to future scholars and to everyone generally interested in Jewish theater.

---

[1]Isaac Bashevis Singer, quoted by Richard Burgin, "Isaac Bashevis Singer Talks... About Everything," *New York Times*, 26 November 1978, VI, p. 24.

[2]Irving Howe, "The Yiddish Theater: A Blaze of Glory and Claptrap," *New York Magazine*, 9 February 1976, pp. 31-38.

CHAPTER

1

Jewish Theater Through The Ages

Ran Avni, artistic director of the Jewish Repertory Theater, likes to say that the JRT is not a replica of Yiddish theater, particularly stereo-typical Yiddish theater, but that it emerged in the 1970s with a new kind of voice, different from anything in the past.

Granted that the Jewish Repertory Theatre's voice is unique, but it did not spring, full-grown, like Athena from the brow of Zeus. Its roots reach into the past, connecting with ancient yearning and expression, running through the centuries into modern times. Jews have always been drawn to theater, even while their religious leaders inveighed against the practice. The proscriptions existed because of the attraction.

Nor was the JRT born in a 1970s vacuum, unaffected by surround-ings and events. In truth, the climate was highly conducive to ethnic theater, and spawned innumerable groups—both Jewish and non-

Jewish—the JRT among them. In short, there have been factors, horizontal in space as well as vertical in time, contributing to the creation and continued existence of the Jewish Repertory Theatre.

The profile of Jewish theater which I present in this chapter is necessarily brief, indicating only the milestones, as it were, and giving a panoramic view. My purpose is to set the stage for the advent of the Jewish Repertory Theatre, pointing out the factors that led to its emergence in the 1970s. For a complete treatment of the history of Jewish theater, I refer the reader to Nahma Sandrow's *Vagabond Stars* and David Lifson's *The Yiddish Theatre in America*.

EARLY JEWISH ATTITUDES TOWARD THEATER

In America Jewish theater experienced its Golden Age at the turn of the century, with a rich, passionate Yiddish theater that was catapulted into the limelight and flourished for a brief fifty-year period. But that theater was centuries in the making, its complex tradition developing in many different forms and places.

In antiquity there is little evidence of Jewish theater, but there must have been some dramatic attempts that warranted the religious proscriptions that existed even then. Biblical writings indicated that theater was viewed as a lewd pastime and heathen practice allied to the worship of false idols, a practice that included the wearing of masks and costumes and assuming make-believe characters. The Old Testament clearly forbids the making of graven images and the male wearing of women's clothes,[1] although the latter may have been inveighing against homosexuality rather than theater. The Old Testament also, according to writer David Lifson, says, "I thank Thee, my Lord, that I spend my time in the temples of prayers instead of in the theaters."[2]

Yet, as time went on, Jews were aware of and influenced by classical and Hellenistic Greek culture. And they were drawn to one of the Greeks' crowning achievements—theater. Jewish religious leaders saw Greek theater for what it was—a religious practice. And if indeed Greek theater stemmed from the Dionysian mysteries, it carried a credo far removed from the Jews' own belief in monotheism and morality.

Although there is a paucity of evidence of Jewish theater, there is one surviving example of a playwright influenced by the Greeks.

In *circa* 150 B.C., Ezekiel of Alexandria, a Jewish poet, emulating Euripides, wrote a play about Moses and other Biblical figures called *Exodus*.[3] There is, however, no indication of any performances.

There was more than religious proscription working against the development of Jewish theater. Jews in the Diaspora, coping with persecution and insecurity, had to be concerned mainly with survival. There is, nonetheless, evidence of Jewish theater development during the Christian era in Europe. Jewish performers parallelled the wandering bards and street entertainers of the Christian medieval world, performing in the Yiddish vernacular for their own people. The *badkhonim* (itinerant musicians and professional jesters) performed outdoors:

> ...traveling groups of entertainers used to give street performances for donations. Since the performance was in the open air, there was no admission charge. These entertainers were half beggars, organ grinders, and acrobats. Their occupation was seasonal; thus they were obliged to beg for their livelihood when the weather was bad for open-air performances.[4]

In time they performed in wealthy Jewish homes for special festivities, giving more skilled and elaborate performances.

THE PURIMSHPIL

The more significant beginnings of Jewish theater, like its Christian counterpart, were to be found within the religion, beginning with the questions and responses in synagogue services, and evolving into the Purim plays *(Purimshpil)*. The one time when Judaism permitted gay festivities was during the early spring festival of Purim, commemorating the Old Testament story of Esther. The Purim story lent itself to theatrical interpretation: Haman, prime minister to Ahashuerus, King of Persia, plots to kill all Jews in the Kingdom. But the king falls in love with and marries a beautiful Jewess named Esther. She, with her cousin, the wise, elderly Mordecai, foil Haman's plot, save the Jews, and Haman is hanged on the very gallows that he had prepared for Mordecai. Purim was a time for wild, joyous festivities, a time when religious restrictions were relaxed and everything could be turned upside down, much like the Christian All Fool's Day. Gravity gave way to drunken revelry, fools held sway over wise men, humble laborers played the role of community leaders.

The reading of the story of Esther began in the synagogue in the fifth century A.D.[5] Gradually moving outdoors, such stories evolved into a people's theater, developing, like the *commedia dell'arte*, stock characters and a strong element of humor. Besides the story of Esther, other Old Testament stories, such as those of Moses, and of David and Goliath, provided plot material, as did secular material borrowed from other theaters. Nahma Sandrow cites a 1588 play, *The Scholar and the Devil*, which was a version of the Faust story.[6]

The widespread dispersion of the Jews in Europe accounts for efforts in different languages:

> While Yiddish plays were developing in Germany and other parts of Central Europe, plays in Hebrew were being given in Italy and among the Spanish Jews in Holland. The first Hebrew play to survive is *The Comedy of a Marriage*, ascribed to Leone di Somi.... The introduction to the earliest extant manuscript of 1618 says that the play was intended for presentation at Purim.[7]

But Jewish theater grew far more slowly than other European theatrical activities. It remained unsophisticated and seasonal until well into the nineteenth century, held back by both the precarious, wandering life of the Jews and their own religious proscriptions.

Another limiting factor was the Yiddish language itself:

> Yiddish was considered a mere *jargon*, unfit for literary use. Until the mid-nineteenth century, a Jewish intellectual in Middle or Eastern Europe used German, Polish, or some other tongue for his literary efforts...Hebrew was too sacred a language for secular plays or even most other secular uses, and, anyway, only the more learned spectators would have understood it. The result was that until the nineteenth century there could be no Yiddish playwrights and no serious Yiddish drama.[8]

THE STAGE IS SET

After this brief introduction to the centuries of sparse theater activities, we move to the focus of this chapter, which is the flowering of Jewish theater—the nineteenth-century Yiddish theater. By the last century, the stage was well prepared for this Golden Age. To begin, the eighteenth century had seen the beginnings of reform and enlightenment for the Jews, launched by the German-Jewish scholar Moses Mendelssohn. The purpose of the *haskala* (a Hebrew word meaning "enlightenment") was to encourage Jews to break away from their intensely narrow lives and to become aware of modern European culture.

> Moses Mendelssohn made it his life work to break the barrier that separated his people from the world. In an age when science, progress, and the brotherhood of man were not seen as separate entities, but as a single new ideal for all mankind, Mendelssohn believed that, armed with a secular education, the Jew, remaining a Jew, would take his rightful place in world culture.[9]

Mendelssohn and his fellow intellectuals saw Yiddish as a lowly dialect, but were willing to use it to reach their co-religionists, and they saw "dramatic literature as a effective weapon."[10] However, most European Jews of that period lived, not in an enlightened western Europe, but in Eastern Europe, within the Tsar's Pale of Settlement, in straitened, isolated circumstances. There the new movement met strong opposition from Orthodox Jewry, and it would take another hundred years for the *haskala* to make inroads. But by the nineteenth century the body of literature in Yiddish and Hebrew was extensive, exposing eastern European Jews to the mainstream culture.

With the enlightenment came a secular life. Wine gardens and inns proliferated in Eastern Europe, and, with them, the appearance of the *Broder* singers—spiritual descendents of the early minstrels and street entertainers.[11] They composed and performed their own songs and wrote timely, satirical monologues, in a language that spoke directly to the people.

At the same time, another powerful movement significant for Yiddish theater swept through Eastern European Jewry—*hasidism*. In contrast to the *haskala*, *hasidism* was a religious movement, a revolt against the rigid established Orthodoxy and one that used the popular arts to make its point.

> It glorified spontaneous song and dance as expressions of joy in the divine. It encouraged the creation of simple lyrics in the vocabulary of the masses.[12]

But it would be some time before all the disparate elements would merge to form a true theater. In 1826, for example, Solomon Ettinger wrote *Serkele*, a tearful comedy about bourgeois family life, in Yiddish. The play was published in 1861, first performed by amateurs in 1863 and staged professionally in Odessa in 1880. Nahma Sandrow explains the time-table:

> In developing beyond folk plays, Yiddish theater followed a general pattern that had occurred in Western Europe in the Renaissance but reached Eastern Europe centuries later. In every case, the "high" drama of an intellectual elite merged gradually with the "low" folk theater to produce a modern national theater... whereas in other cultures the entire process extended over centuries, in Yiddish it was telescoped into one generation.[13]

Yiddish theater would emerge from a combination of efforts and circumstances, including not only the *haskala* writers, the *hasidic* songs and dances, the Purim plays, the *badkhonim*, the *Broder* singers, but also the historic factors of Russia itself.

In 1855 Tsar Alexander II came to the throne. Determined to modernize his country, the young ruler put into effect sweeping changes, and, within his first year, the serfs were freed, the censorship relaxed, and reforms were initiated in every phase of government. As restrictions were lifted, the Jews, most harshly oppressed of all the minorities, benefited greatly. Jewish children were no longer drafted into the Tsar's army at age twelve for twenty-five year stints, but came under the same conscription laws as other Russians (conscription at age eighteen). The special Jewish tax was abolished, and Jews were admitted into Russian universities and into the professions. Under such circumstances, the *haskala* flourished.

In 1876 the Bulgarians revolted against the Ottoman Empire, and the following year the Russians, in a burst of Pan-Slavic feeling, declared war against the Turks. Rumania, too, soon joined the conflict, entering on the side of the Russians. Jassy, in Rumania, became an important communications center during the war, and thousands of Russians flocked to the town, seeking their fortunes.

ENTER GOLDFADN

In 1876 Avrom Goldfadn also came to Jassy, hoping to find work as a journalist. A product of the *haskala*, he had been sent to a school which emphasized western culture as much as Jewish studies. He was a poet, songwriter, and journalist, but he had yet to succeed in any field. His attempts at teaching, publishing, medical shool, and business all ended in failure. But in Jassy he was to find his destiny—to assume the role that has come to be acknowledged as his—the father of Yiddish theater. Stories vary as to how Goldfadn launched the first Yiddish theater company. His own autobiography states that, shortly after his arrival in Jassy, he visited a wine garden to hear a noted Broder singer named Israel Grodner.

> The thought occurred to him that the material would be much more interesting if it was integrated into a play, as he had seen in non-Yiddish plays in Western Europe, Rumania and Russia. He sent for Grodner and they were off.[14]

The team's first effort, a two-act sketch put on in a tavern, was so successful that Goldfadn immediately began to grind out plays. His early plays were little more than plot outlines, scenarios that he handed to Grodner and Grodner's boy assistant.

> The little company, which Godfadn later described as an actor and a half, operated like the Italian *commedia dell'arte*, with which Yiddish folk theater has so many original similarities. Goldfadn made up the plot, wrote the songs, and explained to the actors the characters they were to play.[15]

The plays, says Sandrow, were not great literature, but many were emotional, lyrical, and comical:

> They tap the communal sources of Purim play, folk song, and poem, and they channel that energy into a more complex form. Unlike most of the Yiddish dramatists who rapidly appeared to compete with him, Goldfadn remained true to his source. Thus many of his plays have a freshness, energy, and theatricality which time has not diminshed.[16]

Goldfadn not only wrote, but also directed, produced, and

promoted the shows. Though he lacked theatrical training, ''he gave his audiences what they wanted—a mixture of song and dance, with plots and music borrowed from all over Europe.''[17] With his success, he moved from short sketches to full-length plays, writing about 400 himself. He soon enlarged his little company, employing women on stage for the first time in Jewish history and taking his company on tour throughout Eastern Europe, wherever there were Yiddish-speaking audiences. Like Hollywood moguls of a later age, he was a temperamental dictator, but he created stars—and names such as Sigmund Mogulesco, Jacob Adler, and Sophia Goldstein would become famous. He eventually settled in the United States in 1903, where his plays continued to draw audiences until his death in 1908.[18]

Other would-be entrepreneurs soon entered the field, with Grodner himself, for example, leaving Goldfadn and teaming up with playwright Joseph Lateiner. Many who had their start with Goldfadn revolted against his authoritarian, paternalistic style and set off on their own. In short order, a number of troupes were touring the countryside, performing in *shtetls* (Jewish villages), towns and cities wherever Jews lived.

But the golden era of European Yiddish theater soon ended. In 1881, Tsar Alexander II was assassinated by radicals. Ironically, the very tsar who had introduced sweeping reforms was killed for not effecting change quickly enough. While the radicals thought that the tsar's assassination would bring about a revolution, the reverse, in fact, happened. When the murdered tsar's son, Alexander III, ascended the throne, he brought back a cruel, reactionary regime. For the Jews, particularly, the new regulations were harsh.

> In 1882 the May Laws forced more and more Jews out of the countryside into congested city slums. The quotas of Jews allowed to study were reduced, and Jews were evicted from the practice of their professions. The entire Jewish communities of Moscow, St. Petersburg, and Kharkov were marched in manacles to the railway stations and expelled.[19]

In such a climate, waves of pogroms swept across the Pale of Settlement, adding to the Jews' miseries. As to the actors, an 1883 law banned Yiddish theater entirely, making it impossible for them to work legally in the profession.

YIDDISH THEATER IN AMERICA

Jews, millions of them homeless and destitute, began to emigrate, some settling in England. With them came the actors, and they created a vibrant Yiddish theater in the East End of London, catering to a teeming Jewish population. But the theater was short-lived, as Jews learned English, assimilated, and turned to mainstream English theater. Moreover, the theater suffered a drain of talent, as the Yiddish actors headed across the Atlantic. Opportunities seemed far greater in America, with its burgeoning immigrant population.

Between 1881 and 1903, 1,300,000 Yiddish-speaking Jews arrived in the United States, and most of them settled in the port where they landed—New York City.[20]

Yiddish theater, reaching its full heights in America, would be truly a people's theater, catering to the needs and tastes of the masses. As David Lifson explains, the early immgrants were of three types:

...first, the elderly religious people who spent their time in synagogues and frowned at the theater; second, the intelligentsia who pursued learning and the professions, who encouraged and joined labor movements; and finally, the uneducated workers who were backward and illiterate, but made up the majority of the Yiddish theater audiences.[21]

Exactly when the theater was launched is uncertain, but Boris Thomashevsky is generally acknowledge to be the founder of the Yiddish theater in America. According to one story, as reported by Sandrow, Thomashevsky, a young teen-ager in 1882, was working in a cigarette factory with Abe Golubok. It developed that the young Golubok had two brothers, actors, living in London. When the brothers, destitute and unemployed, wrote to their American brother for help, it was Thomashevsky, a fledgling entrepreneur fired by the idea of theater, who raised money for their passage.

The first show, with the Goluboks and Thomaschevsky, was a failure. The producers decided upon Goldfadn's operetta, *The Witch*, starring a professional actress, one Madame Krantsfeld. They rented Turn Hall on East Fourth Street, hired a 24-man orchestra, and went into rehearsal. The uptown German Jews were horrified that their ragged co-religionists were making a spectacle of themselves and tried to dissuade them. Nevertheless, the show opened as planned, on 18 August 1882, to a full house. But the leading lady was not to be found. The overture was played over and over while the producers rushed to her house:

> There she lay on a sofa, in a kimono, a cold towel on her head. She had a headache. They begged her, they pleaded. It became clear that the committee (the German Jewish Committee) had bribed her to ruin the show. Frantic, they offered money too. When their offer reached three hundred dollars cash down, plus setting Mr. Krantsfeld up with a soda-water stand on the corner of Division Street and the Bowery, she got up, got dressed, and walked with them to Turn Hall.[22]

But it was too late. The chorus, musicians and most of the audience had left.

Despite that first fiasco, Thomashevsky bounced back quickly and soon assembled his own company, adding eager amateurs to his few professionals. He soon had heavy competition as professional and well-known Yiddish companies began to arrive from Europe. Among the early arrivals were Sophia Goldstein and her husband Max Karp and playwright-actor Joseph Lateiner, soon followed by actors Sigmund Mogulesk, Sigmund Feinman, David Kessler, Jacob Adler and Keni Liptzin, and playwright Moyshe Hurwitz. In the time-honored tradition of theater, Thomashevsky retreated to the hinterlands, taking his company on the road, playing Chicago, Philadelphia, and other cities. There he learned his craft, eventually returning to New York to hold his own in the fiercely competitive scene.

Despite the discouragement of the German Jews, Yiddish theater became a thriving enterprise. It served the immigrants' psychological and social needs, replacing the synagogues and the cohesive *shtetl* life of Eastern Europe.

> ...it substituted in subtle ways for the older communal institutions that had been the basis for centuries of Eastern European Jewish life. It was a meeting place, an arbiter of fashion, a common passion. It provided, in the form of actors, popular folk heroes. And it represented loyalty to tradition and to the community.[23]

Moreover, the few hours in the theater provided the immigrants with a glamorous world far removed from their squalid daily lives. Small wonder that they spent their last pennies on theater tickets!

With the constant replenishment of actors and audiences from abroad, American Yiddish theater grew. At its height there were as many as twelve active theaters in New York City, not only on the Lower East Side, but also in Brooklyn and in the Bronx. Companies rose and fell, with competition and cooperation existing side by side. There were constant cross-overs, as producers wooed actors from rival companies. Whole families, like the Thomashevskys and the Adlers, rose to fame.[24]

The Yiddish theater became a world unto itself, not unlike Hollywood of the twentieth century. There were adored stars, and the stars themselves led flamboyant lives. Marriages, affairs, scandals, and battles—all provided exciting gossip for the fans. David Lifson writes that the actors had no artistic pride, bringing their petty quarrels right into the performances and indulging in such stunts as getting married on stage and inviting the audience to join in the ceremony.[25] Since Yiddish theater grew from a *commedia dell'arte* beginning, with actors extemporizing from script plots, it is not surprising that actors, not playwrights, provided the theater's key element. To this day, plays are barely remembered, but actors are recalled glowingly.

The kind of fare that the Yiddish theater offered, at least in its early years, was considered *shund* (trash) by the intellectuals. Moyshe Hurwitz and Joseph Lateiner were the most productive writers, turning out assembly-line plays, including farces, melodramas, and musicals.

> The early immigrant audiences, without esthetic training or experience but with wonderfully avid hungers, have little taste for realism—there is enough "realism" in their lives. What they want is bang-up spectacle, florid declamation, turbulent melodrama.[26]

Shows had to have broad mass appeal—flashiness and novelty. The old country and family life were sentimentalized and great liberties were taken with Jewish history. Working against time, the writers borrowed heavily from many sources, unconcerned about plagiarism or copyright laws, and actors changed lines freely.

The audiences were fervent and uninhibited. They shouted at the actors, munched food, gossiped with friends, read newspapers, and in general carried on their lives openly. At the same time, they were passionately involved in the show—and openly showed their approval or disapproval.[27]

JACOB GORDIN

In the 1890s the theater entered a second phase with playwright Jacob Gordin and actor Jacob Adler. "It [was] a period of extraordinary boldness in adapting classical masterworks to the needs of the immigrant culture."[28] Gordin also introduced a new element, realism, in contrast to the escapist form of theater the Jewish audiences sought, and it would take a while for his dramas to be accepted. He was a journalist and intellectual who had already established a reputation in Russia for his radical views and his fiercely inquiring mind. Soon after arriving in New York City in 1891, he saw his first show on Second Avenue. Disgusted, he vowed to write his own play, which he promptly did. Within a year he had written *Siberia, The Great Socialist*, and *The Yiddishe King Lear*, the latter establishing his reputation and bringing Adler to stardom.

In freely adapting plays by the great European dramatists, in discouraging improvisation, and in "seeking his material in such modern phenomena as the breakdown of traditional Jewish family life under the stress of new surroundings,"[29] Gordin revitalized the theater.

As Lifson summarizes:

> He educated the better Yiddish actors artistically and...he also had a profound cultural influence upon the Yiddish theater audience. Gradually, on both sides of the footlights, there developed an appreciation for plays free from the claptrap of cheap and primitive melodrama.[30]

Gordin's plays, as the intellectuals saw them, were located somewhere midway between *shund* and art. He was a good, but not great, playwright, a serious but not a profound thinker. But he did serve, unquestionably, as a catalyst, a forerunner of the art theater. At the same time his plays provided a moderating influence on the *shund* that continued to appeal to the masses.

YIDDISH ART THEATERS

Following World War I a third phase came into being. At the same time that the Hebrew-speaking Habimah Theatre was founded in Moscow, and, under the influence of Stanislavsky, became world famous for its artistry, Yiddish theater in New York City took a similar turn. A young actor named Maurice Schwartz opened his theater in 1918. Schwartz took over the vacant Irving Place Theater, which had formerly offered plays in German—a commodity no longer saleable in postwar America.

The Yiddish Art Theater, as it was called, had its antecedents in the art theaters launched in the late 1800s in Europe. In addition, Yiddish amateur theatrical clubs, flourishing both in Europe and America, provided incentive. The clubs served as both a source for young actors and a testing ground for serious drama, producing both original works and European plays in translation.

Taking his cue from both sources, Schwartz proclaimed he would open a better kind of theater. With the intimate setting of a small theater, subtler acting would replace exaggeration and bombast. And the company would be an ensemble, with no stars. However, Schwartz seemed to reverse himself by immediately recruiting several top professional actors, among them Jacob Ben Ami, who had been involved with European Yiddish art theaters and dreamed of a similar theater in America. But Ben Ami was destined for disappointment. Schwartz, as it turned out, was, above all, pragmatic—and egocentric. The Yiddish Art Theater would have a well-publicized star after all, none other than Schwartz himself. Schwartz had three criteria for a play, according to historian Nathaniel Buchwald: "first it must be by a familiar author...second, the play must have box office appeal; finally a play must have a strong role for Maurice Schwartz."[31]

Thus Schwartz began to produce traditional Yiddish plays. And though he talked of subtler acting, he himself used the broad style typical of Yiddish theater. According to Lifson, designer Boris Aronson, who worked closely with Schwartz, said that when Schwartz played in the classics, he was a ham, but when he played simple folk-comedy roles, he was magnificent.[32]

Ben Ami finally persuaded Schwartz to let him put on a drama of literary quality. Schwartz agreed to a performance on a Wednesday, usually a slow day. The drama, A Secluded Nook by Ben Ami's friend Peretz Hirshbein, did play to a small audience, but was greatly appreciated, and Schwartz agreed to an extended run. Critics lauded the show, seeing it as a new beginning for Yiddish theater.

But traditional productions prevailed, and at season's end in 1919,

Ben Ami and others broke away to form their own company, which they named the Jewish Art Theater. The dissidents drew up a manifesto, which they subsequently followed, with values closer to the European art theaters: no stars, no one could play a lead twice in a row, no one would refuse smaller roles, and actors would be billed alphabetically. New realistic acting techniques, as developed by André Antoine, Otto Brahm and Konstantin Stanislavsky in Europe and Russia, replaced bombastic style, and serious drama replaced *shund*.

Unfortunately, the Jewish Art Theater, struggling with money problems, lasted a short time, just one season, with its members turning to commercial Yiddish theater or mainstream stage.

Schwartz's theater, though considerably less idealistic, survived until 1950, outlasting Yiddish theater as a whole. His repertoire went on to include not only Yiddish classics (among others, Goldfadn's *Two Kuni-Lemls* and Gordin's *Mirele Efros*), but also the newer Yiddish dramas and the great European dramas in translation. Though members of the company came and went, many were rehired year after year. Schwartz finally built his own theater on Second Avenue and Twelfth Street.

Ben Ami's group was reorganized in 1926-27, running for one season, and other art theaters rose and fell throughout the 1920s, among them the Rudolph Schildkraut Theater, the Yiddish Theater Society and the Yiddish Ensemble Theater.

RADICAL POLITICAL THEATER

A new kind of Yiddish theater emerged in the late 1920s and 1930s, the years of the Depression—politcal radical theater—which paralleled the surge of left-wing political activity in America. The most noted of these companies was Artef (a Yiddish acronym for Workers' Theater Group), which began in 1926 as workers' drama classes sponsored by the *Freiheit*, a Communist newspaper. Artef's goal, according to its first director, Joseph Mestel, was to "build a proletarian theater which would combine Left-Wing ideology but still be rooted in the Jewish heritage. Mestel said that if it lacked the Jewish background...it would lose its strength and fail."[33]

Artef's choice of plays dealt with the Yiddish folk heritage and with workers' problems. It adopted a style which had come to be known in America in the 1930s as "agitprop," theater with a political message.

> The production style that Artef adopted was just then becoming familiar internationally among politically and artistically radical circles...formalist and constructivist, stylized and balletic. Artef's aesthetics, like its politics, were concerned with groupings and mass movement rather than individual introspection.[34]

Despite its self-imposed restrictions, Artef produced a high-level of theater, according to Sandrow.[35] Another politically-oriented Jewish theater of the period was the Yiddish division of the Federal Theatre Project. Directed by Hallie Flanagan under the Works Progress Administration, the Project subsidized some 1200 productions put on by many companies, among them ethnic groups that included Yiddish companies. The Project ran from 1935 to 1939, when it was abolished by Congress because, among other things, it was seen as a form of Communist propaganda.

At the same time, Jewish influence was making its mark on the English-speaking theater, with the works of such playwrights as Elmer Rice, John Howard Lawson, and Clifford Odets. And the Group Theatre was presenting plays of social conscience, some of which focussed directly on Jewish characters and situations. Many Group Theatre members were deeply rooted in Jewish culture. Harold Clurman, for example, was born on the Lower East Side, John Garfield came from a Yiddish-speaking home, and Stella Adler was an offspring of the famed Adler family of Yiddish theater.

AFTER YIDDISH THEATER

But Yiddish theater as a whole began its downward spiral, fading steadily through the period between the two wars. There were substantial reasons for its demise. Eastern European immigrants had been drastically curtailed with the passage of restrictive laws in 1918 and again in the 1920s. The main source of Yiddish-speaking audiences was effectively cut off. Meanwhile attrition was taking its toll. First-generation Yiddish-speaking peoples in America were growing older and dying. The second generation, the immigrants' children, no longer spoke the language. Nor did they have the same needs. With better education, income and jobs, they were entering the mainstream, in fact becoming Americans and turning to English-speaking theater for their entertainment.

The final death blow in the 1940s was the Nazi destruction of almost all Yiddish-speaking European Jews. With it went their communities, way of life, and a rich source of material for Yiddish theater.

But the brief brilliant era of Yiddish theater made its mark on the American cultural scene. It had served as a conduit, to acquaint Americans with new developments in European theater. And, more directly, it spawned a whole new generation of creative people, many of them children of Yiddish theater people. Jewish writers, performers, and producers went on to enhance mainstream American theater and film, and Jewish talents on every level played a role in the creation of the movie industry and the Broadway theater. Unfortunately, it was a role played with little open acknowledgement of their cultural baggage.

> Indeed in the 1930s at the height of Jewish control of the movie industry...there was a concerted effort to ban most Jewish subject matter from Hollywood films. To escape from their Jewish immigrant backgrounds, the moguls eliminated all traces of it on the screen.[36]

While the 1930s were a time of social protest, carrying with it open acknowledgement of ethnicity, the 1940s and 1950s saw a change of attitude, a downplaying of ethnic differences. America chose to see itself as a melting pot, but melted down to the white Protestant image. Such attitudes pervaded the theater world as well. Whatever image of the Jews existed in theater, escapism and trivia were the order of the day—a sharp contrast to the 1930s, when the writers were portraying working-class Jewish and other ethnic families.

Even serious Jewish playwrights avoided ethnic delineation. Neither Arthur Miller nor Lillian Hellman drew openly on their Jewish background, as Sarah Blacher Cohen points out.[37] Their plays may have been subliminally Jewish, but were outwardly sanitized and stripped of such an identity. Even when plays with Jewish themes and characters appeared on Broadway in the 1940s and 1950s, they tended to caricature reality, as in the Broadway productions of H.S. Kraft's *Cafe Crown* in 1942 and Gertrude Berg's *Me and Molly* in 1948.

But the 1960s, a time of major political and social ferment, a time

of new tolerance, a time of theatrical experimentation, provided the
setting for ethnic, and ultimately English-speaking, Jewish theater.
The black civil rights movement paved the way, encouraging political activism and ethnic awareness among such other groups as native
Americans, Hispanics, and Asian-Americans. Theater expressed a
new pride in ethnic identity, exploring its parameters and protest-
ing prejudice and injustices. Not surprisingly, Jewish theater
emerged, as Jewish community centers nationwide formed amateur
theatrical groups to present, in English, works of Jewish themes and
writers.

In such a climate the new professional English-language Jewish
theater, with the Jewish Repertory Theatre in the forefront of the
movement, was born. "Reborn" is a more accurate term, as the current Jewish theater does indeed draw on thousands of years of history. The *Purimshpil* have made their contribution, as have the
badkhonim, Tsar Alexander II, Avrom Goldfadn and the stars of the
Yiddish theater. The nineteenth-century European theater movements, with the art theaters of Antoine, Brahm, Grein, and Stanislavsky, and the works of Ibsen, Chekhov, and Shaw also made their
impact. The social revolt of the 1960s and the new awareness and
acknowledgement of ethnic differences were crucial. Many factors,
coming together in the right time and place, contributed to the birth
of the Jewish Repertory Theatre in 1974. The stage was set.

[1]Deuteronomy, xxii.5

[2]David S. Lifson, *The Yiddish Theatre in America* (New York and London: Thomas
Yoseloff, 1965), p. 18, citing B. Gorin, *The History of the Jewish Theatre* (in Yiddish;
2nd ed.,; New York: Max N. Maisel, 1923), I, 12. I could not, however, find this reference in the Old Testament.

[3]Ibid.

[4]Ibid., p. 21.

[5]Ibid., p. 20.

[6]Nahma Sandrow, *Vagabond Stars* (New York: Harper & Row, 1977), p. 6.

[7]Phyllis Hartnoll, *The Oxford Companion to the Theatre*, 4th ed. (Oxford: Oxford
University Press, 1983), p. 440.

[8]Sandrow, *Vagabond Stars*, p. 19.

[9]Lulla Rosenfeld, *Bright Star of Exile* (New York: Thomas Y. Crowell Company,
1977), p. 33.

[10]Lifson, *Yiddish Theatre*, p. 24.

[11]The name derived from the eastern Polish city of Brod, birthplace of one of their most famous entertainers, Ber Margoles, who was known as Berl Broder, which means "little Ber from Brod." Sandrow, *Vagabond Stars*, p. 37.

[12]Sandrow, *Vagabond Stars*, p. 33.

[13]Ibid., p. 22.

[14]Ibid., p. 41.

[15]Ibid., p. 45.

[16]Ibid.

[17]Hartnoll, *Oxford Companion*, p. 441.

[18]His most famous play, *Two Kuni-Lemls*, produced in Kharkov, Russia, in 1880, enjoyed popular runs in America, and finally reappeared in New York in 1984. Under the title, *Kuni-Leml*, the new English adaptation, written by Nahma Sandrow, became a hit. (See chapters 4, 5, and 6 of this study.)

[19]Rosenfeld, *Bright Star*, p. 57.

[20]Sandrow, *Vagabond Stars*, p. 72.

[21]B. Gorin, *History of the Jewish Theatre* (in Yiddish, 2nd ed.; New York: Max N. Maisel, 1923) I, 12, cited by Lifson, *Yiddish Theatre*, p. 43.

[22]Sandrow, *Vagabond Stars*, p. 75.

[23]Ibid., p. 77.

[24]Yiddish theater flourished primarily in the United States, but existed wherever there were sizeable Yiddish-speaking communities, such as in South America and Europe, providing audiences for American Yiddish stars touring abroad.

[25]Lifson, *Yiddish Theatre*, p. 126.

[26]Irving Howe and Kenneth Libo, *How We Lived* (New York: Richard Marek Publishers, 1979). p. 239.

[27]A century later audiences, revealing their antecedents, would exhibit similar behavior at Jewish Repertory Theatre performances.

[28]Howe, *How We Lived*, p. 253.

[29]Hartnoll, *Oxford Companion*, p. 441.

[30]Lifson, *Yiddish Theatre*, p. 79.

[31]Nathaniel Buchwald, *Teater* (in Yiddish; New York: Fariag Committee, 1943), p. 392, cited by Lifson, *Yiddish Theatre*, p. 332.

[32]Lifson, *Yiddish Theatre*, p. 381.

[33]Lifson, *Yiddish Theatre*, p. 442.

[34]Sandrow, *Vagabond Stars*, p. 281.

[35]Ibid., p. 278.

[36]Sarah Blacher Cohen, "Yiddish Origins and Jewish-American Transformations," *From Hester Street to Hollywood*, ed. Sarah Blacher Cohen (Bloomington: Indiana University Press, 1986), p. 12.

[37] Ibid., p. 7.

CHAPTER
2

The Theater's Early Beginnings

Founded in 1974, the Jewish Repertory Theatre owes its life to the vision of one man. A communal art form such as theater involves many people. of course, but the JRT's conception, birth, and continued growth rests, first of all, with Israeli-born Ran Avni.

Fortuitous circumstances combined to bring about the theater's origin. The time was ripe to launch a Jewish theater in New York City, but Avni also had the motivation and persistence to make it happen.

Avni, settled in New York City in 1974, had travelled a circuitous road over his lifetime of some thirty years that had led from a *kibbutz* in Israel to midtown Manhattan. His story begins at Kfar Menachem, near Ashkelon, a coastal city in the country that was then Palestine. His parents had emigrated from Poland in 1936, and, like other Labor Zionists, were determined to help found a Jewish state based on socialist agrarian principles. They believed that a series of *kibbutzim* (collective farms) would provide the building blocks for the new nation. Like other settlers in Palestine, they embraced a new way of life and a new name, translating their European name of Epstein to the Hebrew name of Avni.[1]

Despite training in Poland at Socialist Zioinst youth camps, the elder Avnis had little preparation for the realities of Palestinian farm life. Nonetheless, Avraham Avni became an expert in the growing of food for farm animals. "With little knowledge of any languages but Yiddish and Hebrew, my father travelled around the world to learn the systems, and he built a mill that serviced the entire south of the country."[2]

The Avnis had three children: Dorit (who is now a social worker in Jerusalem), Benny (now a journalist with *H'Air*, a weekly magazine in Tel Aviv) and Ran, who was born in 1941. The children attended elementary school on the *kibbutz*, where their mother Shulamith was a teacher. Ran was attracted to the theater in his youth. His earliest theatrical memories were those of an eight-year-old, performing in Purim festivals. "I dressed up as Charlie Chaplin, and I remember standing in the circle doing my routine with the cane and shoes backward."[3] Later, he performed in school shows, and in high school (a regional school that served several *kibbutzim*), he helped organize, produce and direct several productions.

Graduating from high school in 1959, he served his two-and-half year stint in the army as a paratrooper and then returned to the *kibbutz*. He remained for a year, torn between staying on (which would have pleased his parents) or leaving home to pursue a career in the theater. The theater won out. He borrowed money from his uncle to buy an accordion, learned to play the instrument, and began to support himself by playing with various musical groups.

He soon enrolled in a three-year acting program at Beth Zvi, a drama school in Ramat Gan. His courses there, in addition to acting, included dancing, fencing, general gymnastics, vocal development, diction, theater history, and play analysis. At school he had the opportunity to perform in European and American classics, including the works of Shakespeare, Strindberg, and Inge. He came under the influence of Fanny Lubitch, a former student of Stanislavsky, whose teaching incorporated Stanislavsky techniques into her own style.[4]

During this time he continued to work, directing army theater groups and teaching drama in high school. He also continued to perform with his accordion and to give lessons on the instrument.

Following graduation from Beth Zvi in 1966, he went immediately into the Cameri Theater, and over the next three years he would work with the Cameri, the Habimah State Theatre, and the Open Theatre (Israel's Off-Broadway theater). All three companies were based in Tel Aviv, but travelled around the country to give performances.

Avni's theatrical career was interrupted when the Six-Day War erupted in 1967 and he was recalled to active service.

> I had been cast in a musical in the Cameri, and I went to
> war during rehearsals. When I came back, I found my
> role had been taken by a fellow name Mike Burstyn.[5]

Avni continued to work in theater, but began to think of further training as a director, possibly in America, a country he yearned to revisit.[6]

He discovered that the Jewish Agency sponsored a program which sent Israelis to America for three-year stints as cultural attaches. He applied, but with the request that he be allowed to study as well as work. The Agency reluctantly agreed, and he was sent to Boston in 1969, arriving with his wife Ora, who also planned to study.

In 1969, his first year in America. he worked at the Jewish Community Center of Brookline-Brighton-Newton as cultural arts director. At the same time, in preparing for graduate school, he took extension courses at Harvard—one course combining philosophy and psychology and the other elements of folklore and theater. For the next two years he continued to work at the Newton JCC and study at Emerson College in Boston, gradually working into a full-time program at the college. In that period, he directed college productions of Federico Garcia Lorca's *The House of Bernard Alba*, Jean Genet's *The Maids*, and Peter Weiss's *Marat/Sade*. In 1972, he completed his master's degree program in dramatic arts, with a major in directing, at Emerson.

Though his daughter Sheerly was born in Boston in 1970, his wife, too, continued to study, receiving a master of arts degree in French literature at Boston University. By the time she was accepted in a Ph.D. program at Yale University, the Avnis had agreed to separate. In 1972 Ora Avni and daughter went off to New Haven, while Ran

Avni turned to New York City, center of the American theater world.

That same year he found a job with the Staten Island Jewish Community Center as cultural arts director.

> I applied for the job, came down for an interview, then
> took a cross-country trip while waiting for the answer,
> I called every other day. I knew that if I didn't get the job
> I would have to go back to Israel. I didn't have a work-
> ing permit or anything. On the last day of the trip I called
> and they said they would take me for a year and would
> apply for my working permit.[7]

Avni was not happy with his job nor with the atmosphere at the Center. The job called for the supervision of many so-called cultural activities that were far afield from theater, and he found himself swamped with administrative chores. The atmosphere, as he saw it, was one that stressed social service and community involvement rather than creativity, ''a social work atmosphere'' as he saw it. But the Center job made it possible for him to stay on in the States and also to develop a drama group. While there, he directed productions of *Oliver, The Sound of Music* and *Barefoot in the Park* with youth and adult groups. He, in fact, stayed at the job from 1972 to 1976, until he had firmly launched the Jewish Repertory Theatre and himself as its director.

In 1973 the Yom Kippur War broke out in Israel, and Avni returned once again to the Israeli army. He came back to the United States after the war in total despair, and, although he surely knew other Israelis in New York, he was alone, single, friendless, as he expressed it.[8] But he was not quite totally lost. The Staten Island job had been kept open for him, and he was able to reactivate the drama group, which was a lifeline to his identity and purpose. Despite the limitations of working with amateurs, he could seek out and produce plays that interested him.

In 1974, looking for a workable play, he stumbled upon the melodrama *God of Vengeance*. It was the best-known play of Sholom Asch, Jewish novelist and playwright. Written in Yiddish in about 1905 and translated into English by Queens College professor Joseph Landis, it was included in an anthology entitled *Five Yiddish Plays*.

God of Vengeance, with its theme of lesbianism and its presentation of Jewish brothels and brothel-keepers, was a shocking play in its time and still makes a strong statement. The story deals with a brothel manager and his wife who attempt to raise their daughter in protective isolation so that she might become the proper wife of a rabbi. (The parallels to Shaw's *Mrs. Warren's Profession* are patent. Mrs. Warren, with her earnings as a prostitute, sends her daughter to the best schools so that she can enter British upper-class society.) But the brothel-keeper's plan fails when the daughter falls in love and runs off with a prostitute.

The play could not be performed in Czarist Russian territory because of the ban on Yiddish plays, but a German translation was produced by Max Reinhardt in 1907 in Berlin. An instant artistic success, it alerted the theatrical world to the possibilities of Yiddish theater and went on to translations and productions in many countries.[9] For Avni, it was a play with a challenge, even for an amateur group:

> It was a kind of a nice piece of drama. I realized I was
> not going to do Shakespeare with the group. But I had
> a production, and I actually had a good time with it.[10]

While the play was in rehearsal, he was approached by a fellow Israeli, an actor named Avner Regev, who said that a foundation was willing to give $200 to a group of Israeli theater artists to start a theatrical activity. Avni suggested they produce his *God of Vengeance*. Regev came to see the show during its one-weekend run and was excited by it. "It was the perfect time in my life to do something totally outrageous—either get killed in the war or something. So I said, 'let's do a production.'"[11] Of course, he was not throwing all caution to the winds. He would continue to keep his Staten Island job.

It was a propitious time to attempt to establish a New York City theater that focussed on the Jewish experience. In a city with a large Jewish population, there were many potential writers, actors, directors, and theatergoers. Also, it was a time when ethnic theater—Hispanic, Black, Oriental, among others—was gaining interest and applause. There was reason to believe that a new Jewish theater would receive support. In fact, when Avni and Regev turned for advice to Alice Spivak, an acting teacher whom Regev knew at HB (Herbert Berghof) Studios, Spivak encouraged them to start a Jewish theater. "In this city, with its Jewish population and the Jewish interest in the arts, you can't miss! Go for it!"[12]

The Avni/Regev theater, in fact, was not created in a vacuum.

There was a long history of Jewish theater in America, and of Jewish contributions to mainstream American theater, dating back to the nineteenth century (as discussed in Chapter 1). But the earlier theater had its own language, Yiddish, to identify it as Jewish. And the direct descendants of the Yiddish theater—the spiritual children of the Yiddish producers, directors, actors—had moved away from Jewish and into mainstream American theater and film, certainly making their impact but not identifying themselves or their contributions as Jewish.

With the return of Jewish theater in the 1970s, the circumstances would be entirely new. The Jewish population as a whole was clearly a part of mainstream America, sharing common language, culture, attitudes—while yet maintaining, to some degree, a Jewish identity. What was it to be Jewish in America in 1974? There were no clear answers. The new Jewish theater of the 1970s would address itself to that puzzling question. Moreover, the new Jewish theater—specifically Avni's JRT—would have its own identity problems. It would not have a unique language to identify its ethnicity. But it wanted to be seen as clearly and deeply Jewish, whatever that might mean, as would its artistic directors, its playwrights and many of its actors and directors. As Ed Cohen writes in a commentary on the JRT begnnings:

> Avni wished to form a theater in which the central issue of the material produced was the 'address' of the characters; not a theater restricted to plays by Jewish playwrights, nor plays with Jewish characters, but one concerned with plays about Jewishness, about roots, their value, the loss of them, the search for them, the distaste for them, the joy of them. This is a truly ethnic theater. Certainly, in New York City, he assumed that such a concept would be valuable.[13]

Avni himself explained his original goals in a later magazine interview:

> "My aim from the beginning was to legitimize Jewish theater," Avni declares. "No longer will we be a stepchild, a poor relation, but an artistic equal." This implies, among other things, no Yiddish accents, no Yiddish comics, no Jewish stereotypes like the Jewish mama. "A well-written play does not need accents," says Avni.

"The writing provides the rhythm and the speech patterns."[14]

Thus, fueled by impulse, by ideals and by a sense of timing, the Jewish Repertory Theatre was born. It was a theater that Avni believed would appeal to Jew and non-Jew alike, if its productions were on a high professional level, and he intended to see that they were.

In the fall of 1974 Avni and Regev rented space at the tiny 60-seat Omni theater on West 18th Street and proceeded to cast the play *God of Vengeance*. They discovered, surprisingly, that several professional actors, for a number of reasons, were willing to work without pay. Martha Schlamme, for instance, who would play the role of the aging prostitute, felt it was an opportunity to act. She had long been recognized as an accomplished folk singer and interpreter of Brecht/Weill music. In point of fact, she had developed a reputation as a singer and found it difficult to get work other than as a singer. People did not think of her as an actress, a fact which she found frustrating and limiting. Schlamme was studying at the HB Studio under actress Uta Hagen, as was Regev, and Schlamme responded eagerly to the Avni/Regev project. The cast also included Lillian Lux, veteran actress of Yiddish theater, who was looking for just such an opportunity at the time. Ultimately, the cast would include five Equity players: Patrick Farrelly, Etain O'Malley, and Paul Rosson, as well as Schlamme and Lux. The non-Equity players were Regev, Magdalena, Lucille Mahon, and Wendie Marks.

Martha Schlamme recalled that the production, in rehearsal, had its problems. There was strong conflict between Lillian Lux and Avner Regev because of their two very different styles of acting. Regev, like Schlamme, was being trained in Stanislavsky techniques by Uta Hagen, encouraged to act from the inside out, to become the character, as Schlamme put it. Lux, on the other hand, came from the old Yiddish theater tradition, where the idea was "to show the audience." In the Yiddish theater tradition, of course, acting meant using a declamatory or grand style. Schlamme explained:

> Lillian would direct Avner in the middle of a scene when they were acting togther. While he was acting, she would interrupt and whisper to him. He would have a fit. Avner had a terrible temper. It was nervous-making for the rest of us.[15]

Nonetheless, the end result in October 1974 was a production that worked and was appreciated by the small number of viewers and critics who saw it. Schlamme remembers Avni as a good director, who mediated and remained calm and pulled the production together. Debbi Wasserman, writing for *Show Business* on 17 October, commented that "as a first effort, *God of Vengeance* is a satisfying one and offers promise of finer things to come."[16] She added that the JRT's avowed purpose was to present plays with Jewish themes that have meaning for every one and that "despite some rough spots, their first production clearly adheres to that goal."[17]

Wasserman was indeed impressed with the performances of Schlamme, Lux, O'Malley and Farrelly, but less so with the other performers and with Landis's somewhat stiff English translation. David Lifson, however, writing for the *Gramercy Herald* on the same day, felt that the Landis translation was "vigorous and excellent."[18] As to the performances, Lifson thought that Schlamme was the outstanding performer, in fact brilliant, demonstrating "a deep and vast reservoir of dramatic talent." Lux and Regev were also first-class, he said. But the non-Jewish Farrelly was miscast, because, in Lifson's view, no one but a Jew could handle the role. "The cadence, the mannerisms, the very being of Jewishness is demanded from this role—and all are lacking."[19] *Hadassah Magazine*, on the other hand, felt that the Farrelly performance was powerful, with equally polished performances from Lux, O'Malley and Schlamme. As to the direction, despite "poor use of stage movement," the magazine indicated that Avni's concepts were sound, the play built solidly, and the company was off to an impressive start.[20]

The production ran from 10 to 27 October 1974 and must be considered, on balance, a critical success. But it was hardly a financial success. The entire production cost between $600 and $800, with the money coming from Avni's and Regev's pockets. Regev's hoped-for funding never materialized. In all, there was a profit of $6.22, after the directors were repaid.[21]

But for Avni, it was a totally exhilarating experience. For the first time he had worked with professionals; trained actors responded to his directives. Whatever the problems and limitations of the production, it proved to Avni that he was, at last, where he belonged.

Pleased with its reception, Avni and Regev accepted an invitation to take the show on the road, transporting it to the Jewish Community Center of Southern New Jersey in Camden, New Jersey, for a single performance in December 1974. It proved to be a disaster. Avni says:

> I learned my lesson—that theater doesn't transport well. We took this little show and its sets to a gym that seated 900 people, and the sets didn't cover a third of the stage. It was simply horrendous.[22]

That winter, the two co-founders were taking the next step—searching for a permanent home for the JRT. They needed space, at minimal cost, where they could rehearse and put on productions. Avni found an old building on West 42nd Street (the area that would later become Theater Row), which included an abandoned theater and an adjoining restaurant called "Jaffa." Both were owned by a man called "Moish," whose full name Avni never was able to learn. According to Avni: "He agreed to let us use the theater and gave us a deal where we would pay him half the box office instead of rent."[23]

The place had no heat and had been left a shambles. But with youthful determination and optimism, they proceeded at once to the task of housecleaning, beginning with the office. However, when they arrived the next day, they found "real workmen with real tools" at work tearing down walls. They rushed to Moish for an explanation. He replied casually, "Some people came and offered me $10,000 for the theater, so I couldn't refuse."[24] The people in question were the founders of Playwrights Horizons. They had received a grant, and it was the start of the now-famous Theater Row and a permanent home for Playwrights Horizons. For Avni and Regev, it was a bad setback—although a temporary one.

Avni began to seek out a Jewish institution, possibly a community center, which would have space and facilities. He approached synagogues, unsuccessfully, and then the 92nd Street Y successfully, but felt that the basement space they offered was inadequate. Finally in November 1974 he wandered in off the street at the Emanu-El Midtown YM-YWHA on 14th Street and approached Don Geller, executive director. Would the Y be interested in housing a professional theater? Geller said that he would indeed like to have a Jewish theater, that it was within the framework of what his organization should be doing. "It met a variety of the goals of the Y in terms of culture and Jewishness,'' said Geller.[25] But unfortunately he had no theater facilities. Avni persisted, asking to see what space was available. Geller showed him a bare low-ceilinged room, with an adjoining kitchen, on the Y's second floor. The room, which he called a lounge, was used for dance classes and other daytime activities but was free evenings. Avni felt a sense of excitement when he saw the room. Later he described his reaction in the following manner:

> It had advantages. It was not just off the street. It would
> not be noisy. The kitchen could be the lighting booth....
> Perhaps these classrooms could be dressing rooms. And
> some day that room could be an office.[26]

But to Geller, he said only, "It has possibilities. We'd need a platform for audience seating but, with a minimum of change and cost, we could put on a production."[27]

Geller of course knew nothing of Avni's full intentions at the time. It was only later, dealing with the JRT on a daily basis, that he learned that "theaters swallow up space."[28] For the moment, Geller was intrigued but primarily concerned with the cost of setting up a theater. Moreover, such an innovative and important project would have to be submitted to the the Y's board of directors for approval. Avni submitted the necessary information to him, and Geller wrote a proposal which he presented to the board. Geller's request was understandably vague, dealing with a theater that was still more fantasy than fact. He wrote:

> We have been approached to participate in some fashion
> with a Jewish Repertory Company [sic]. The company
> was organized by Mr. Ron [sic] Avni, an Israeli.[29]

But he pointed out that the company intended to maintain high artistic standards and would present plays of Jewish themes and flavor, plays of literary value and meaningful content. The initial outlay would be $600 to $750, to cover the costs of platforms, curtains, light, and such capital costs. Hidden expenses would include additional maintenance burdens and added administrative responsibilities. Admission tickets to the shows would be $3.00 and $4.00, with the Y keeping 30 percent of the box office gross. The JRT would use the remaining money to pay its production costs.

It was understandable that Geller was drawn to Avni's plans for a theater and that he thought the board would be favorably disposed as well. A theater was not an inappropriate activity for the Emanu-El Midtown YM-YWHA, which already had a sturdy program of cultural acitivities. The Y was a busy, bustling neighborhood community center with dance, music, arts and crafts programs, a center for seniors, a Hebrew school, a nursery school, a photography gallery, and a health club.

The board did in fact see the theater as an appropriate addition, but, exercising caution, approved it on a one-time trial basis. It wanted to see what kind of fare, and what level of fare, the theater would provide, and it wanted to see what audience response there would be. Thus the JRT had its temporary quarters—quarters that have remained a home base to the present. Recalling those early days, Geller says, "I confess I didn't think we would be ten years down the road and still here."[30]

Geller claims that it was the chemistry of Avni and himself working together—discussing, planning, negotiating,—that made it possible. "I guess, without either one of us, the JRT would not be here. That is clear."[31] Regev, he says, played a minor role in the negotiation and disappeared from the scene at an early point in JRT history.[32]

Over the next few months, the minimal structural changes that Avni required were put in place, with much of the manual work accomplished by the founders themselves. The kitchen was converted into a light and sound booth. Ceiling tiles were torn down so that lights could be installed. Temporary audience platforms (to be taken down after each performance) were placed on three sides of the room, thus creating a floor-level thrust stage. The platforms could seat 100 spectators and gave audiences raised seats looking down on the stage. Avni recalls:

> There were such problems. If I'd had any kind of wisdom or ability to foresee the problems, I might have given up before I ever started.[33]

One difficulty was that the Y's maintenance men saw the theater as merely additional work. For example, at one point Avni was standing on a ladder, determining how to install the overhead lighting. A fight broke out among the maintenance men surrounding him. Avni recalled,

> One of them threw a screwdriver, and it hit me in the

back of my leg and I started bleeding. It was such a metaphor for what my entire struggle with the theater would be.[34]

By midwinter, nevertheless, the fledgling theater was completed, but the proper play was yet to be found, and it would not be until May of 1975 that a production would be on the boards. Avni thought to himself with chagrin, "I've caused all this commotion and now I don't have a play!" But eventually Regev found a play that Avni liked, an Israeli one that had been translated into English—*Lady of the Castle*—by the Israeli poet Leah Goldberg. Avni believed it would be a new experience for Americans, a good reason to produce the play. He states:

> I had seen the play in Israel, in Hebrew, and recalled it was a success there. But I had a stronger reason for choosing it. I had felt from the very beginning that it was important for us to do plays that were rarely produced, revivals and translations, in addition to new plays.[35]

Though the play was by an Israeli writer, its milieu is a central European country. It deals with the search for orphaned children after World War II and focusses on one young Jewish girl who was hidden by a count in his castle. The play explores the attitudes of surviviors of the Holocaust and their difficulties adjusting to new realities in the post-war world.

Once again, Avni would direct the production and Regev would play one of the roles. Actors from the HB Studio, where Regev studied, would fill the other three roles. The cast finally included Elise Hunt, who was studying with Uta Hagen, and Lynn Polan and Paul Rosson (who had performed in *God of Vengeance*), both from Alice Spivak's classes. Seeking a young woman to play the key role, Avni went to a Spivak class and discovered the two likely possibilities: Lynn Polan and Tanya Roberts. He auditioned both, and chose Polan for the part.[36] It was the beginning of an enduring important professional relationship for Avni and Polan and would take Polan from an acting to a directing career. Polan, Avni still feels, was a fine actress and the best choice for the role of the young girl. But he was less satisfied with the other performers (Avner Regev and Paul Rosson in the male roles) and recast the other female role with Elise Hunt a week before opening night.

Lynn Polan's recollections are also that the cast was not very good.
She says:

> Avner Regev may have been a good actor, and was hard-
> working, but his accent was difficult. It was the second
> show the JRT had ever done, and no one knew who they
> were. It's not so easy to get people to work free. I was
> willing because I wanted the experience. [37]

For Polan, it was a major breakthrough—her first important role
in a serious play, although she had played roles in musicals. It was
an experience she describes as both terrifying and wonderful. As a
director, Avni tended to be abrupt and straightforward. She says:
"I think I really wanted somebody to be sweet, and I was rather fright-
ened by him." [38] But she adored her role, she says, and remembers
the whole experience fondly. It also regenerated her sense of Jewishness. Coming from a mixed Jewish background, she had been
raised as a Jew, but lost contact with it during boarding school and
college days, "where it wasn't cool to be Jewish." [39] Preparing for
the role, she researched the historic setting and events. "It awakened
all kinds of things that had been dormant for years." [40] She also recalls
that the set was a low-budget effort with furniture thrown together
by the maintenance men. She claims:

> It looked it. They probably spent twenty-five bucks on
> the set. It was really a minimal set. It was supposed to
> be the rich elegant library of a European castle, but it
> looked like somebody's basement where they did carpen-
> try. [41]

By the time the show opened, the JRT had made different financial arrangements with the Y. The 30 percent plan had been dropped.
The Y would keep all box office receipts, but also pick up all expenses. It was the only way, Avni realized, that the JRT could keep
afloat at that time. But expenses had to be kept to a minimum. There
was little money for sets or props, none for actors. Polan says: "We
were not even given subway fare for that first show." [42]

Nor was Avni, the director, paid. Nor Avni, the set designer. Nor
Avni, the set builder. (Avni would, in fact, be unpaid for the next
two years, keeping his Staten Island job, until the JRT reached a certain level of recognition.)

Box office returns for *Lady of the Castle* were certainly not gratifying throughout the three-week run. The show had had little publicity, and few knew of the JRT debut. Polan recalls:

> The largest audience we got was 25 people. We had some
> nights when we were not sure we should do the show,
> with fewer people in the audience than in the cast.[43]

There are no official records of the box office returns, but Don Geller confirms, from his own memory, that returns were poor. It was only after that he would begin to keep records and grow more sophisticated with JRT record-keeping.[44] Few critics appeared to cover the event (no one from the major dailies), and those few who did gave the show subdued reviews. *Hadassah Magazine*, for example, pointed out that the cast did not equal that of the JRT's first production, but it praised Regev's performance.[45]

Yet, despite such an inauspicious beginning, the JRT survived, with the blessings of Don Geller and the Y board of directors, and it presented a full season of plays in 1975-1976. Both the advantages and difficulties of the theater's connection with the Emanu-El Midtown Y were already apparent that first season, factors that would plague and bless the JRT through the years.

To begin with, the Y employees (such as maintenance men and office workers) neither understood nor were interested in professional theater. They did not take the JRT seriously. As far as they were concerned, the theater was one more Y activity that they found to be a nuisance and additional work. They gave grudgingly and often incompetently of their services. Phone calls and messages that came into the Y's main office, for example, frequently never reached the theater people, particularly that first year. Avni had to fight step by step for the necessary services, losing as many battles as he won. And even Don Geller, who had helped to launch the theater, did not give it preferential treatment over other Y activities, in terms of space or funding. The theater would have to be satisfied with makeshift quarters, shared with other groups, and with minimal outlay for productions. Moreover, Ran Avni was constantly in a position of approaching Don Geller, palm outstretched, for theater needs. It was not a comfortable stance for the co-founder and director of the JRT.

On the other hand, the JRT had a secure, rent-free home. It also had free services in terms of heating, lighting, maintenance, carpentry, publicity, box office, ticket-printing. It had the identification with a Jewish Y that would help audiences to accept it as a Jewish theater, a factor that would be instrumental in building audiences. And it had the backing of the Y board, willing to pick up the deficit that was as inevitable with the JRT as with any other non-profit theater. In the world of off-off-Broadway theater, where theaters operate on a shoestring, the JRT had more financial security than most. In all, though the JRT had a humble beginning in 1975-1976, its first season set the pattern for the years to come.

---

[1]In German, *stein* means "stone"; in Hebrew *Avni* means, literally, "of stone," a name that would serve as both a metaphor and a prophecy for the founder and director of the JRT. Only someone with the endurance of stone could have survived the stormy ten-year history of the JRT. He would build a theater as his parents had helped build a *kibbutz* and a nation.

[2]Ran Avni, interview, New York City, 5 February 1985.

[3]Ibid.

[4]Avni claims that Lubitch recognized his strengths, that she said he could be "a good actor or a wonderful director" and that he should choose between the two.

[5]Burstyn, who is today a popular American actor, was living in Israel at the time, with his parents Pesach Burstein and Lilliam Lux, stars of the Yiddish stage. Avni and Burstyn would meet again in America in 1985 when both helped organize the first annual Goldie Awards in Jewish theater.

[6]When he was six years old, he and his mother had paid a brief visit to her sister, who worked for the United Nations and lived in Parkway Village, an international settlement in Queens, New York.

[7]Avni, interview, 5 February 1985.

[8]Ibid.

[9]E. Harris, "Asch, Sholom," *Oxford Companion*, ed. Hartnoll, p. 47.

[10]Avni, interview, 5 February 1985.

[11]Ibid.

[12]Alice Spivak, interview, New York City, 31 May 1985.

[13]Edward M. Cohen, "The Jewish Repertory Theatre: A Subjective Account," New York City, 1979. (Mimeographed article available at the JRT offices.)

[14]Hannah Grad Goodman, "Just Off Broadway," *Hadassah Magazine*, November 1984, p. 59.

[15]Martha Schlamme, interview, New York City, 20 February 1985.

[16]Debbi Wasserman, "God of Vengeance," *Show Business*, 17 October 1974, taken from the clipping files of the Jewish Repertory Theatre, as are all following reviews in this and subsequent chapters unless otherwise noted.

[17]Ibid.

[18]David Lifson, "Spotlight on Theater," *Gramercy Herald*, 17 October 1974.

[19]Ibid.

[20]"An Anglo-Jewish Theater," *Hadassah Magazine*, November 1974.

[21]Avni, interview, 5 February 1985.

[22]Ibid.

[23]Ibid.

[24]Ibid.

[25]Don Geller, interview, New York City, 16 September 1986.

[26]Avni, interview, 5 February 1985.

[27]Ibid.

[28]Geller, interview, 28 March 1985.

[29]Don Geller's proposal to the Board of Directors, Emanu-El Midtown YM-YWHA, December 1974. Geller had yet to learn the correct titles and names.

[30]Geller, interview, 28 March 1985.

[31]Ibid.

[32]Avner Regev continued to be part of the Jewish Repertory Theatre, appearing on the program as executive producer and performer until February 1976 (see Chapter 3). Known for a volatile personality, he had difficulties with Geller and other Y officials, according to Avni, and finally left after the production of *Andorra*. According to colleagues, he remained in New York for the next few years, studying at the HB Studio, before moving on to the West Coast. Alice Spivak has heard from him on occasion, and Avni claims to have seen Regev in character roles on film. But unfortunately he has been impossible to trace, and his recollections of the early JRT, which would have been invaluable, cannot be included.

[33]Avni, interview, 5 February 1985.

[34]Ibid.

[35]Ibid.

[36]Roberts lost the part but went on to television and movie fame, including a part in the successful television series, *Charlie's Angels*, and the starring role in the James Bond movie, *A View to Kill*.

[37]Lynn Polan, interview, New York City, 5 April 1985.

[38]Ibid.

[39]Ibid.

[40]Ibid.

[41]Ibid.

[42]Ibid.

[43]Ibid.

[44]Geller, interview, 28 March 1985.

[45]"Choose Life," *Hadassah Magazine*, June 1975.

The Years 1975 to 1980

THE FIRST SEASON—1975-1976

The first full year for the Jewish Repertory Theatre was 1975-1976. That year the fledgling company presented four productions: September—*A Night in'May*, November—*Relatives* and *The Closing of Mendel's Cafe* (two one-act plays), February—*Andorra*, and June—*East Side Justice*. Each play ran for four weeks for a total of twelve performances. The JRT, at that point, had an Actors Equity showcase contract, which permitted Equity actors to work without pay (carfare only) but gave them freedom to leave at any time for other offers. The contract limited the number of performances to twelve and the seating of the theater to one hundred. The JRT shows would be given on Thursday and Saturday nights and Sunday matinees. The theater was dark on Fridays because of the Jewish Sabbath.

The JRT continued to be a modest, underfunded operation that year, with gradual moves toward professionalism. There was little money for props, sets, designs, and no money for people involved in the production. Set designers and actors were recruited from schools; i.e., they were students who were still learning their craft and willing to work for experience in lieu of salary. Props, such as furniture and other house furnishings, were often "found objects," pulled in from the neighborhood streets or borrowed from friends' apartments. As to other needs, the facilities of the Midtown Y (on East 14th Street), with its maintenance and office staffs, were available, supposedly, to the theater company. But their availability was often more theoretical than actual, as the JRT had to compete fiercely with the demands of other Y departments.

During the summer of 1975 Avni continued to work for the Staten Island Jewish Center, running its summer cultural activities program and, at the same time, planning for his new Jewish theater on 14th Street and for its first full season. Looking for play material, he turned again to the anthology of Israeli plays that had offered *The Lady of the Castle*. He focused on *A Night in May*, by A.B. Yehoshua and translated from the Hebrew by Miriam Arad. He had seen and enjoyed the drama in Israel years earlier, where it had considerable critical acclaim. The play, dealing with the anguish of a modern Israeli family caught up in war, was a subject to which Israeli audiences could well relate.

Avni and Regev realized that Avni could not direct every play, and Regev suggested a woman director named Ann Raychel whom he knew through the Herbert Berghof (HB) Studio. With *A Night in May*, Raychel became the JRT's first outside director. She recruited several competent actors, including Anne Pitoniak, who ten years later would win a Tony nomination for her Broadway performance in *'night, Mother*. Other Equity players included Dorothy Fielding, Brandwell Teuscher, Evelyn Tracy and Katherine Mylenki. Regev appeared in the play, as did two fellow HB students: Shanit Keter and Peter Von Berg.

Lacking set designers or crew, the founders directed the maintenance staff to build a crude set. Acoustics were poor because of the old ceiling, and, show by show, members of the company removed ceiling tiles. Moreover, the theater space continued to double for dance classes, and the maintenance men were instructed to convert the room from dance studio to theater as needed. Rarely was the assignment carried out, and Avni was plagued with the constant last-minute problem of setting up platforms and chairs for each show. Avni recalled:

> The last dance class ended at 5:45 [P.M.], right as the maintenance crew shifted, and every Thursday I would find myself at about 6:00 P.M., running from Staten Island with my blood pressure going up, knowing the platforms would not be up. Don Geller [executive director of the Y], by that time, was already in Brooklyn. I was left literally every Thursday with a bunch of drunken maintenance men and nothing set up. I had to get the platforms up, get the chairs on the platforms, and make sure the broken chairs were in the back row![1]

Despite such crises, the JRT's first show of the season opened each night on schedule throughout the month. Avni looked back on the production as adequate but not wildly successful. As he saw it, the production had some good actors and an "okay director."[2] The audience did not respond well in terms of filling the house. The only really successful evening (in fact a sell-out) was a benefit performance for an Israeli student organization. Consequently, Avni discovered that plays do not necessarily translate from one culture to another. *A Night in May* had won both the Israel Drama Critics and Harp of David awards in Israel, but American audiences, and critics as well, were far less enthusiastic. With little understanding of Israeli attitudes and feelings of patriotism, they saw the play as soap opera.

Both the *Village Voice* reviewer and Jennie Schulman, reviewing in *Backstage*, were negative. The *Voice* reviewer said:

> I found it very interesting at moments and maddeningly tedious at other moments, and it's really difficult for me to get a sense of what the playwright...is talking about....
> I came away with no discernible point of view; the work seems to be more about making scenes happen than trying to understand something about people in a society at a critical moment.[3]

Critic Schulman agreed:

...either the playwright hasn't written a very convinc-
ing play or the translation from Hebrew into English lost
the play's thread.[4]

But *Hadassah Magazine*, a Jewish publication, reviewed the show
sympathetically, calling it "an illuminating work on a meaningful
theme, and we must be grateful for the chance to see it."[5]

In November the JRT featured two new one-act plays by an American writer, Eve Abel, under Avni's direction. Abel had sent her plays
to Avni upon reading one of his ads in the trade press. Avni read the
plays and found them intriguing. The first play, *Relatives*, is a short
two-character drama dealing with a young man who is trapped be-
hind a rock. His uncle passes by, hands out advice and philosophy,
but does not help to free him. The second play, *The Closing of Mendel's Cafe*, is the story of a middle-aged mediocre violinist who earns
his living playing in a cafe but is faced with a personal crisis when
his job ends. Both plays are concerned with the limitations of life and
circumstances in which people find themselves ensnared.

Once again, the cast was composed of more Equity than non-Equity
actors, with five Equity actors and three others. Again, HB Studio
was a source of supply for actors. Playing the leand in *Mendel's Cafe*
was Equity actor Sheldon Feldner, who had been Avni's teacher at
Emerson College. Initially, Avni found it strange to have the roles
of teacher and pupil reversed, with himself auditioning and directing his former teacher, but both adjusted to the situation. Lynn Polan
appeared in her second JRT show, playing two roles in *Mendel's
Cafe*, and Michael Mantel, playing the young man in *Relatives*, began his long association with the company. Like Polan, Mantel was
a student at HB Studio.

Mantel was not happy with the play nor with his co-actor, Paul
Rosson, but he was pleased to be working, particularly for Avni,
whom he found open and approachable. The theater itself was, he
thought, "more cafeteria than theater, very makeshift," but typical of the off-off-Broadway theaters in which Mantel had worked.
The audience, too, at that point, was limited. "Sometimes it felt like
the cast was bigger than the audience, and the cast was two."[6]

This production was still very much a shoestring operation. Total
production expenses for the show added up to $275.22, which in-
cluded such items as "$15.00 for cast party," "$6.00 for fabric for

couch,'' and ''$1.90 for silver hair spray.'' Modest though the operation was, it had its share of crises. One late night after rehearsal the playwright found herself locked into the dark building. She had apparently gone to the bathroom and emerged shortly, to find that the actors had left and all doors had been locked. She managed to get to a pay telephone in the building and called the fire department.

A more serious crisis for the production itself was the tape recorder incident: music was critical to *Mendel's Cafe*, because the lead charater spends his time reminiscing and presumably playing his violin. Avni achieved the effect with taped synchronized music, and for that purpose had found an old, somewhat unreliable tape recorder. On the day that Don Nelsen, critic from the *Daily News*, was scheduled to attend, the recorder broke down. Avni turned to Geller in a panic, but Geller assured him that one of the maintenance men would repair it.

> At 6:00 P.M., when I came running from Staten Island,
> on top of the regular problems, the tape recorder was not
> fixed. Besides, Gregory, one of the drunkards, had
> opened the whole recorder and couldn't put it back
> together. He told me a story about a missing part.[7]

Ultimately, Avni was forced to appear on stage and explain to the audience that an important element was missing that night. ''Unfortunately, the tape recorder is not functioning, so just imagine the music,'' he said, thinking he had found a brilliant solution.[8] But the critic found the explanation neither brilliant nor satisfying. When an actor called to ask why his review had never appeared, Nelsen explained that the show's standards were poor and he thought it was a ''Y drama group.''[9] Although ignored by the *Daily News* as well as other New York mainstream newspapers, the plays did have one somewhat favorable review in the New York Jewish press. Elenore Lester in the *Jewish Week-American Examiner* commented:

> The playwright reveals sensitivity, humor and a good ear
> for common speech. However, she fumbles in her effort
> to grasp the essential dramatic strands.[10]

Avni's choice for the February 1976 production was *Andorra* by the Swiss dramatist and novelist Max Frisch, a tale about latent bigotry and the factors that bring it to light. Frisch, who served in the Swiss army, draws on his own experiences and reflections, and, though Andorra is a mythical country, it could be any European country in the twentieth century—a somewhat mythical country with its Jewish scapegoat.

The team of Anne Pitoniak and Ann Raychel appeared again, with Pitoniak playing a pivotal role and Raychel directing and casting faculty members from HB Studio who were seasoned actors. The drama was also the first production to have a designed set, designed by Dennis Hearn, also an HB Studio acting student.

It was also the last JRT play for one HB student—Avner Regev. Although Regev did not perform in the play, he was still listed on the program as executive producer. But differences with Avni, with Geller and others led to his departure shortly thereafter. As Avni explained it, Regev was an actor, not a producer or director, and actors, particularly those whose primary interest was acting, do not head up companies.[11] But a greater difficulty may have been Regev's explosive personaliy, which sometimes led to angry scenes with Geller and others.

The play was the most successful of the season, with the largest audiences and best reviews, although the reviews were still confined to the Jewish press and a small paper. *Hadassah Magazine* commented fairly favorably:

Andorra is a powerful and disturbing play. Its selection as JRC's [sic] fifth vehicle maintains the group's high standards in plays. It also demonstrates the company's ability to attract very good talent for their showcase productions. . . . The play and the cast surmount the production's clumsy direction, which fails in all the key scenes.[12]

Valerie Owen, on the other hand, found the entire production "top-notch," including the direction, acting, and technical aspects. As to the set, she said:

The white platform set pieces, hanging diagonal designs, the uncovered linoleum—all keep us from getting too comfortable. The play is mounted like a photo exhibit in a hard-edged painting of reality.[13]

But the linoleum was not a stroke of creative genius. "It was left there because Don Geller would not let us touch the floor because of the dance classes."[14]

The company's final show of the season, in April, with Avni

completely in command, was *East Side Justice*, a play based on true cases of the Jewish Conciliation Board (popoularly known as the Jewish Court).[15] Initially, it was the interest of Alice Spivak that led to *East Side Justice*. "I wanted to do the 'Bintel Brief,' because I recalled my mother writing a letter to them."[16] The "Bintel Brief" was the famous letter-to-the-editor column in the Yiddish-language newspaper, the *Jewish Daily Forward*. The material had been shaped into a book entitled *A Bintel Brief*, edited by Isaac Metzker, who worked on the newspaper. Both Avni and Spivak saw the dramatic and human-interest possibilities, and Avni approached Metzker. Metzker explained that another producer already had the rights, but he suggested an alternative. He had another weekly column based on cases of the Jewish Conciliation Board. Both Avni and Spivak were delighted. The cases, with their built-in conflict, had even more dramatic and human interest possibilities than the letters to the editor. Metzker, with a strong writing background that included not only his work on the *Forward* but also five published books in Yiddish, selected the cases and, with the help of his wife, who was once his student in a Yiddish class, translated the material. The result was a sequence of separate scenes, but, as it turned out, a play without a unifying structure.

The cast included Spivak and Sy Travers (both Equity actors) in the adult roles, with Lynn Polan and Robert Farber (both Spivak students at the time) in the youthful roles. "I played everything from a little old lady whose belongings had been stolen in a grocery store to a woman suing for breach of promise. I loved it."[17] For Polan, it was a third appearance at the JRT. She felt comfortable enough at that point to make strong suggestions to Avni, as he recalled:

> At one point I thought we should make the audience the judges, giving them ballots and having them vote their decisions at the end of each scene, but Lynn said it was too gimicky and convinced me not to do it.[18]

Only a few reviewers covered the show and those few were negative; Metzker's own paper praised Spivak but not the theater, which it saw as "only a room."[19] Nancy Kelton, too, liked Spivak, but not the play:

> While these stories might make interesting copy in a magazine or newspaper, they do not work as a play.

There is not enough conflict or substance and what hap-
pens on stage is of little consequence.[20]

Only *Hadassah Magazine* was essentially sympathetic:
East Side Justice suffers from long narrative introduc-
tions and from windups told in the third person. But the
individual scenes are well-written, and the picture of the
life of immigrants and their American-born children
earlier in this century is thoroughly enjoyable.[21]

The end of the first year revealed that the JRT had increased its
attendance and gate with every show except the last. It was the first
year that Don Geller kept records, and information was still sparse—
but to the point. *A Night in May* had earned $388, and *Relatives* and
The Closing of Mendel's Cafe, with 377 attendees, accrued $611.

Andorra proved to be the biggest box office success of the year,
with 473 theatergoers and a gate of $974. Its success may have been
due partly to the name of the playwright. Swiss dramatist Max Frisch
had a solid international reputation, and, while his name was not a
household word in this country, the JRT production could have attracted serious students of theater. It was a rare opportunity to see
Andorra. But, more likely, the success was due to the size of the cast.
JRT audience, at that time, were comprised mainly of the cast members' families, colleagues, and friends, as the theater had yet to gain
recognition in the larger world. A larger cast therefore produced larger audiences.

The final play, *East Side Justice*, with its lack of a known
playwright and its small cast, attracted only 400 people and earned
$499. One-third the total number of seats were filled by holders of
complimentary tickets, which of course added nothing to the gate.

The season saw the end of the Avni-Regev partnership, with
Regev's departure and Avni's installation as sole artistic director.
(Avni would steadily maintain that sole control over its ten-year history and up to the present, although others, such as Betsy Imershein
and Edward Cohen would be added to the staff from time to time,
and Don Geller and Alfred Plant would provide advice and guidance.)

In all, 1250 people had seen shows at the JRT that first full season, which brought in total receipts of $2472. Although Geller
claimed to have no way of knowing what the JRT actually cost him,
since most of the JRT expenses were part of the overall Emanu-El

Midtown YMHA upkeep, he felt that JRT expenses far outweighed their income. Geller was not happy about theater expenditures, and he would never learn to live with them comfortably, as they increased steadily with each subsequent season, even as the gate increased. But he accepted the financial burden because he viewed the JRT as a valuable, appropriate and prestigious addition to his institution.

THE SECOND SEASON—1976-1977

That summer Avni continued to work at Staten Island, directing a cultural arts camp he had founded for young people interested in the arts. But it would be his last days with the Staten Island Jewish Center. He left at the end of the summer, and proceeded to live on his unemployment checks for the upcoming season, since he was yet to be paid at the JRT.

Avni recalls the period as one of the happiest of his life. He subsisted on a pittance, but, as he explains, his needs were modest and expenses were limited. He had sold his car, which he no longer needed, since his Staten Island commuting days were over. And he had inherited a rent-controlled Manhattan apartment from a friend. Most important of all, he was free to give all his time to the JRT. Many of the problems with the Y staff and the theater space persisted, easing only gradually, but Avni had more time to cope with them.

Avni convinced Geller that he needed an office, and he was given a tiny room wedged between the boiler room and the Y's swimming pool. Despite his exposure to the heady chlorine fumes on one side and the intense boiler heat on the other side, Avni forged ahead.

He planned an ambitious 1976-1977 season, with six productions, but as it turned out, only five were staged. In the spring of 1977, the YMHA was involved in a labor dispute, and the spring production had to be cancelled. The shows of 1976-1977, the second full season, included: Paddy Chayevsky's *Middle of the Night* as the opener, followed by *Jonah, Cafe Crown, The Condemned of Altona, Cakes with the Wine* (cancelled while in rehearsal), and *Ivanov*.

Anvi discussed the possibility of a Chayevsky play at length with Alice Spivak and others. Spivak suggested *Gideon*, which did not appeal to Avni, or *The Tenth Man*, which he felt had been overdone. His final choice was Chayevsky's first play, *Middle of the Night*, because it had been produced so rarely, and Avni recalls that he was easily able to get the rights from Samuel French.

He advertised in the trade journals for a director, and, from the resumes he received, chose Martin Zurla, who was then directing a play off-off-Broadway. Avni explains, "One of the attractive things about him was that he was also a designer."[22] And Zurla would indeed design and build a substantial two-level set, moving well beyond the previous makeshift sets.

The play, which deals with the love affair of an old Jewish man and a young non-Jewish girl, had opened on Broadway in 1956. It played for two years, with Edward G. Robinson and Gena Rowlands in the leads. In the JRT revival about half the cast were seasoned Equity players, with Murray Moston and Maggie Flanigan in the leads. Although Avni had been cautioned not to do a show over the Labor Day week-end, that no one would attend, he did open that week-end. Whether it was the Chayevsky name, the charm of the play itself, or the production, the play was a success, selling out both its Saturday night and Sunday matinee performances. The total audience was 797, the largest figure up to that time.

But the event was not without disaster. The JRT had been rehearsing during the late summer weeks. Don Geller was on vacation and his assistant Sandy Kahn, a social worker, was in charge. Avni asked her if they could have access to a van used by he Society for the Deaf (an organization that occupies one floor of the Y). He and Zurla needed to bring in heavy props and furniture. After much negotiation, Kahn managed to procure the van, but warned them, as they drove off, not to get into an accident. As they returned, pulling up in front of the Y, Avni, who was driving, commented upon how easy it was to drive a van. With that, he opened the door, and a passing car smashed into the door.

Avni recalls that when Geller returned from vacation, he (Avni) rushed in to tell him about the Labor Day weekend sell-out. But Geller, pale and shaken, could only ask, "What did you do to the van?"[23] According to Avni, Geller had a thorough-going tantrum, cursing and stamping about the office and never once mentioning the success of *Middle of the Night*.

Despite audience approval, critics were more circumspect. Sy Syna of *Wisdom's Child*, a New York neighborhood publication, found the play heart-warming, with solidly-portrayed characters. He also praised the casting, but felt the directing was out of control, with the cast given far too much freedom.[24] Shelly Uva of the *Eastside Courier*, another neighborhood paper, was clearly critical:

> The Jewish Repertory Theatre production is in trouble
> on all levels. The staging of the play is clumsy and dis-
> tracting and the lighting is simply atrocious. Many of the
> company's...performances range from one-dimensional
> and boring to mannered and cliched.[25]

And Eleanore Lester of the Jewish press found the play dated and full of cliches, but ably directed by Zurla.[26]

In late October the JRT moved on to the musical play *Jonah*. It evolved when Avni, looking for directors, contacted Chuck Selber, a writer and director. Selber, a southern Jew, arrived with a play he had written called *Mahzel Tov, Y'all*. The play, he admitted, was not ready, but he did have the rights to another play, a Biblical parable called *The Sign of Jonah*. The play, dealing with Germans and their guilt after the Holocaust, was written by a German pastor, Guenter Rutenborn. Avni recalled:

> I wasn't crazy about it, but it was intellectual, had an aura
> of importance, was based on the Bible, and dealt indirect-
> ly with the Holocaust. Perfect![27]

Selber adapted the drama into a musical and directed the production, bringing seven Equity actors to the cast of ten. The play had excellent advance publicity, with blurbs in the *New York Times*, the *Sunday News*, *Show Business*, and *New York Magazine*. Consequently the show sold out for Sunday matinees, and Avni, at the request of the actors, extended the run for an extra Sunday evening performance. ''The whole idea was that agents were coming to see the genius actors,'' says Avni. ''I had nothing to gain.''

In point of fact he had a lot to lose. One of the actors told the union that Avni had, in violation of the showcase contract, extended the show. Avni was brought up on charges before Actors Equity and was fined. He had to turn over the final week's box office receipts to Equity. Although Geller wondered if they indeed had to honor the fine, Avni explained that it was important to maintain their Equity status. He had already arranged for Allen Swift, who would be his first star, to do his next show, *Cafe Crown*, and he did not want to jeopardize that opportunity. Avni learned from the *Jonah* experience that Equity was a force to be respected, that its rules were not to be taken lightly. At the same time, however, it was one more crisis in a crisis-ridden business, and Avni was used to meeting crises on a daily basis. *Jonah*, despite its success with audiences, was ignored by the critics, except for a brief comment in *Show Business*, which criticized the acting and singing but thought the show was worth seeing.[28]

Avni, however, was right about his December show, *Cafe Crown*, which he himself directed. It was to be his first certified hit, playing to sell-out houses and bringing in over $2000 in box office receipts, JRT's largest earnings up to that point. Announcement of the show had appeared in the ''Going Out Guide'' of the *New York Times*, which may have helped. Avni recalled seeing the newspaper listing as he headed downtown via subway for his unemployment check. Sitting on the subway, he had a moment of elation.

Cafe Crown, written by H.S. Kraft and produced on Broadway in the 1940s, is a nostalgic comedy about the old Yiddish theater. All the action takes place in a Jewish restaurant on Second Avenue,[29] where the actors meet, dine, negotiate deals, and socialize. At the center of the action is David Cole, one-time star of the Yiddish stage. Avni's revival featured veteran television and stage actor Allen Swift and a cast of twenty actors, most of them Equity players. Avni recalled that it was difficult to cast them because ''you have to cast a bunch of old Jewish men. But I got middle-aged men. It was a lovely play, and we all had a ball.''[30]

It was also the JRT's first review in a major New York paper— not a favorable one, but a write-up all the same. Ernest Leogrande of the *New York Daily News* found the play ''a period piece, remote in relevance,'' concluding that ''the action sputters rather than snaps.''[31] However, both *Show Business*[32] and *Back Stage*[33] thought the show worth seeing.

Avni found and assigned a new outside director for the February play—Jean McFaddin (who later went on to become special events director for Macy's). He was impressed with McFaddin's credentials, which included work as a director, designer, administrator and producer in regional theaters, as well as in New York City and Europe. They decided upon the Jean-Paul Sartre play, *The Condemned of Altona*, partly because, Avni said, he fondly remembered the movie with Sophia Loren, Frederic March, and Maximilian Schell. But other factors may have been at work. The play deals with the theme of guilt and concerns a German family haunted by its past involvement with Hitlerism. Avni may have been drawn intuitively to the play's exploration of guilt, a theme so common in Jewish drama that it could be considered the definitive Jewish theme.

McFaddin rounded up an able cast, bringing back Anne Pitoniak and including the noted actor Stefan Schnabel. Schnabel was a respected veteran performer, with some forty years of experience in theater (both classics and contemporary plays), radio (over 3000 broadcasts), and television. Schnabel recalled the experience happily: "We had good actors, and Avni was a charming, cultured, civil person, nice to work with."[34] Schnabel felt that the location had its drawbacks, with walking down 14th Street late at night "a little hairy," and the theater space itself, with its noisy air-conditioner that drowned out the actors, difficult but probably no worse than other off-Broadway houses.[35]

Despite the battery of talents, plus advance billing in *New York Magazine* and *The New York Post*, audiences did not respond to the Sartre drama. It may have been that word of mouth of those who had attended, or the lack of reviews, kept people away. Although Sartre is a towering figure in the world of ideas and the play provided a forum for the exploration of his existential philosophy, the play lacked emotional impact. Its character simply did not come to life. A *Village Voice* review tended to agree:

> Despite the presence of a series of good performers, the work is stuck within attitudes, within theatrical posturing, as one performer after another takes center stage to proclaim an idea or verbally challenge someone else. It is the old Gallic ailment at work: theory triumphant over concrete reality.[36]

The dearth of reviews was very disappointing to the actors. They had received no money and had worked for the exposure and good notices, said Schnabel.[37]

The next production, Edward Cohen's play, *Cakes With the Wine*, was scheduled for April. But, as it turned out, it was not performed because of intervening labor problems at the Y. However, this play would mark the beginning of Cohen's association with Avni and the

JRT. Cohen, who at that time was connected with Playwrights Horizons, had adapted the play from his own novel called *$250,000*. Avni recalled:

> He sent me a script out of nowhere. It was the first, real,
> full Jewish play, showing Jews as they are, Jews from
> a poor Jewish neighborhood. Ed had credits, and the play
> was kind of provocative. So I said, "Fine. Let's do it."[38]

But other factors interfered. While the play was in rehearsal, the union at the Y was negotiating a new contract for its office and maintenance people and was threatening a strike. The management subverted the strike by locking out the workers on April 20, the very night before the show opened. In retrospect, both Cohen and Avni felt that the play and production had had many problems and it may have been "a blessing in disguise" not to have produced it.[39]

The lock-out dragged on, but Geller assured Avni that it would be settled by June, in time for the next JRT play. The JRT went into rehearsal for Chekhov's *Ivanov*, directed by Don Marlette, rehearsing in a rented theater space at the Westbeth Theater and in apartments. It was not until a week before the June opening that the production was rehearsed at the JRT.

Marlette had been recommended by Lynn Polan, who knew him from the HB Studio and had seen him direct. He brought along his own group, mostly HB Studio students, who would provide a nucleus for future JRT productions. Ray Smith was assistant director, Pat Lawler stage manager, Mark Spergel (a Ph.D. candidate in theater at the City University of New York) as assistant stage manager, and Lynn Polan and Michael Mantel were in the cast. Later Marlette would bring in Adalberto Ortiz as set designer.

Ray Smith, who is now a writer/producer for the television show "Today," recalls the experience fondly:

> We often rehearsed at a Riverside Drive apartment, and
> it created a closeness, so Chekhovian. The alliances from
> the apartment seemed to work in the play. It brought a
> feeling of ensemble that, to this day, I haven't felt since.[40]

Autonomy also contributed to the group's closeness, according to Smith:

> The good thing always about Ran Avni was that once he

hired you, you didn't see him until the end of the rehearsal period. That's how our little group formed, because we had autonomy. We stayed together and grew together.[41]

Mark Spergel, too, remembers a wonderful time:

I had a bit part and didn't have to work that hard, but it was a real pleasure to work on. Don did wonderul things with that play.[42]

But there were difficulties with the theater space. Once the Y reopened, the last week of rehearsing the cast of eighteen went forward at the Y, often taking place in the nursery room. At other times, rehearsals were scheduled for a classroom, and actors, upon arriving, would find a class in session. There was no storage space, and the cast had personal items stolen.

Smith says that out of necessity they themselves made changes in the theater:

There was no cooperation from Don Geller, but we made changes. Pat and I got Ran to take out the false ceiling, which caused the lights to shine right in the actors' faces. Don Geller had a fit about that, but it gave us two more feet. And we were the first ones to paint the floor black, to denote the stage area.... And the place was so filthy we couldn't stand it. We literally used to clean the bathrooms.[43]

The group also convinced Avni to present *Ivanov* in the round, instead of the proscenium form he usually used. They felt that having the actors enter from all parts of the room gave a greater feeling of ensemble.

Ivanov deals with the breakdown of one man within the nineteenth century Russian rural society. It is the story of a young aristocratic Russian landowner, saddled to an ailing wife he no longer loves, a woman who is a social outcast because she is Jewish. Moving at Chekhov's usual slow pace, it offers careful insight into an array of characters and their interpersonal relations and is also a commentary on Russian rural society and attitudes toward Jews. An early Chekhov play, it shows a glimmer of future Chekhovian strengths, but tends to be over-wordy and structurally weak. Nevertheless, critics responded well to the JRT production. Linda Stein said:

This play has the spark of genius that illuminates Chek-

> hov's later mature works, and it can be brought out by
> a deft production. The Jewish Repertory Theatre is do-
> ing a lovely job with it now.... The acting has depth and
> sensitivity.[44]

Elenore Lester felt that the production needed swifter pacing, but
that director Marlette kept good control over the play's complexi-
ties.[45]

In all, the 1976-1977 season marked significant progress for the
theater. It was the year that the JRT began to find its true audience.
Friends and relatives of the cast had comprised previous audiences,
but, with *Cafe Crown* the JRT began to build a solid neighborhood
audience. It was Avni's first certified hit, covered by a major New
York newspaper, with his first well-known actor, Allen Swift. And
the following production brought Stefan Schnabel, another noted actor, to the JRT. Avni was, at last, in full control, and his operation
and productions began to take on a more professional look. Both attendance and gate receipts had picked up in the second full season,
ending with a gate of $7156 and total attendance of 3466.

THE THIRD SEASON—1977-1978

That summer Avni returned to Israel for a visit. But he already had
plans under way for the 1977-1978 season: Cohen was assigned to
direct S.N. Behrman's *The Cold Wind and the Warm* for the opening show, Avni had Julius Landau's script in hand, and Don Marlette
was slated to direct another show.

As it turned out, Avni produced six plays that season: *The Cold
Wind and the Warm, Dancing in New York City, The Merchant of
Venice, Anna Kleiber, I Am a Camera,* and *I Am a Zoo.* Avni directed
only one of the six.

He returned from Israel to see the Behrman play in rehearsal, with
a cast of twelve, staged by Cohen. *The Cold Wind and the Warm* did
not get a strong reception and was almost overlooked by the critics.
It deals with the Jewish immigrant experience in America and the
pain of adapting to a new culture. But Debbi Wasserman, the lone
reviewer, wrote:

> On one level, it is a tragic tale of Willie, a young, modern
> intellectual, in love with the wrong woman; on another
> level, it is a Jewish mystical play.... The JRT production

works quite well on the first level, but gives us only a hint
of the second.[46]

Avni directed the second play, which opened in December 1977. It
was a work of a new playwright, Julius Landau, who had sent his
unsolicited play to Avni. In *Dancing in New York City* Landau had
created a Jewish ''Marty,'' dealing with six middle-aged bachelors.
Avni was pleased with the production and the cast. His only difficulty
lay in the last-minute replacement of a lighting designer.

Dancing would prove to be a delight to audiences—and to critics
as well:

> Author Julius Landau sensitively sketches the world of
> middle-aged singles, where all live on emotional food
> stamps which stave off starvation but satisfy none....Ran
> Avni underplays humor and pathos, directing the profes-
> sional cast to act so simply they might be real people.[47]

Hannah Grad Goodman adds that the play, a wry comedy of man-
ners and mores, hits a nerve, and that Avni directs with humor and
insight.[48]

Dancing also marked the official beginning of Betsy Imershein's
career with the company. Imershein had graduated the previous June
from Yeshiva University with a master's degree in social work. While
in graduate school she had worked as a social work graduate student
at the Midtown YMHA. The experience was a disaster, she recalled,
an experience saved only by her contact with the theater and her ripen-
ing friendship with Ran Avni.[49] After graduation from Yeshiva, she
worked briefly as a social worker in a state psychiatric hospital in
Brooklyn, but still maintaining her contact with the theater. The theater would prove to be more compelling and congenial than social
work.

She proceeded to spend more and more time at the theater, helping out in any way possible. When the original stage manager for
Dancing quit, she took over the job. It was an exciting debut. ''The
play consistently sold out, and it was the beginning of a different kind
of audience, a different generation, for the JRT. I loved it,'' she
said.[50] She gradually took on more of the business management
chores at the theater, freeing Avni to concentrate on the artistic side.
At the same time, she did office work elsewhere two days a week
to support herself.

Edward Cohen was also spending more time at the theater, reading scripts and giving Avni his evaluations of plays and productions, a contribution that Avni would come to value more and more. Cohen sifted through scripts carefully, weeding out the best. He worked cloesly with the writers, editing scripts and making suggestions for rewrites.

That winter saw another major change. Alfred Plant came on the scene in the newly-created post of chairman of the board of the Jewish Repertory Theatre. Plant was a former president of the Board of Directors of the Emanu-El Midtown YMHA and had continued to serve on its board. But he had recently retired as an advertising executive and had more free time for pursuit of other interests. Geller convinced him that his time woud be well spent assisting the theater.

> At that time there was no board, no chairman, just Ran
> Avni and Don Geller overseeing it. They were operat-
> ing literally on a shoestring but they were managing to
> produce six shows a year, some very important worth-
> while shows.[51]

Plant began by considering what the JRT was meant to be. He realized that it was not just another off-off-Broadway theater, but had a different purpose. The statement of purpose, which he wrote, made it clear that the theater would not be all things to all people, but that it should continue to present plays about Jewish culture and values. The statement reiterated what Avni had always felt, but placed it in written form.

Plant's next order of business was to establish a JRT board of directors. Through a friend at the Television Academny name Martha Greenhouse, Plant recruited such notable performers as Anne Jackson, Eli Wallach, Howard da Silva, Anne Meara and Jerry Stiller. Also included were singer Martha Schlamme and actress Gerry Lou Silverman. The board, as Plant explained, added prestige rather than working hands. The theater continued to function by small committee, with Avni aided by Geller and Plant, and with Cohen and Imershein playing key roles. Plant's major role would be as fund-raiser, and he managed, by the spring of 1978, to have collected $1000 each from Grey Advertising Agency, Readers Digest Association, the DeWitt Wallace Fund, the Columbia Broadcasting System, and the American Broadcasting Company, as well as other contributions.

In February of 1978 the JRT went on to produce *The Merchant of Venice*, directed by Jonathan Foster, who took the unorthodox approach that Shakespeare's classic was a romantic comedy, not a tragedy of an old Jew.

The JRT was not the first to revive the drama in the 1970s, nor to give it a non-traditional interpretation. The Royal Shakespeare Company's 1972 production in London stressed the play's commercial aspect, portraying all its characters as greedy and ambitious. And the glittering, modern-dress version of Ellis Rabb, staged at the Vivian Beaumont Theater in 1973, offered up a herioc Shylock that exonerated Shakespeare from anti-Semitism. Clive Barnes did not buy it:

> It is difficult to us to accept it, but Shakespeare was not only a male chauvinist pig, he was also an anti-Semite....Mr. Rabb tried to give a more sympathetic Shylock than the play can easily sustain.[52]

The JRT's primarily Jewish audiences accepted the company's production with remarkably little criticism of the play's themes and characters, adding no fuel to the debate on Shakespeare and anti-Semitism. Avni himself did not see the play as an anti-Semitic tract. The way to do the piece, he felt, was to examine the reasons for Shylock's behavior. "Shakesepare's approach was not to show that Jews were bad but that Jews did bad things because of the circumstances they were in."[53] But, beyond that, Avni accepted Foster's lighthearted interpretation: "After Shylock's speech, every one had a good time. So what's wrong with that?"[54]

Critics too, liked the approach, though the play was not the sellout of its predecessor. John Bush Jones saw it as a sprightly, vigorous comedy, "a veritable showcase for the multi-faceted talents of its director," and a provocative reading of the play that works.[55] Curiously, the *Village Voice* reviewer saw it as a "simple, straightforward and obvious production," and pointed out, "Such an unimaginative staging of Shakespeare is a rare and wonderful treat."[56]

The 1978 spring play, *Anna Kleiber*, marked the return of the Don Marlette group which had worked so successfully with *Ivanov*. Marlette had wanted to do the drama by Alfonso Sastre, a playwright well known in Madrid but little known in this country. The story of a Spanish actress and her corruption during World War II, the play's only connection to Jewish issues is its Nazi milieu. It would be one of a number of plays at the JRT that had dubious credentials as a Jewish play, such as *The Condemned of Altona* the previous season or the later *Lilion* by Ferenc Molnar and *The Matchmaker* by Thornton Wilder.

Marlette brought in, not only Ray Smith as assistant director, as well as actors Michael Mantel, Mark Spergel and others who had joined him in the earlier producton, but also the young set designer Adalberto Ortiz.

The play's musical effects were provided by a quartet, with Ran Avni delightedly returning to the accordion.[57] The set, which was unanimously considered brilliant, involved a huge swastika as a backdrop and caused at least one theatergoer to leave in a fury.

But JRT audiences were known to behave peculiarly—or at least differently from other audiences. Like Yiddish audiences of old, they talked out in the middle of scenes and stomped out of the theater if they disapproved. It established a rapport and a reminder of the past that some Jewish actors enjoyed, but which Smith found distressing.

> They would talk to the actors and yell out what they thought the ending would be. And, on one occasion, then the lights went out, they shouted and made kissing sounds. It was very disconcerting to the actors.[58]

In all, *Anna Kleiber* was an experiment, but not a successful experiment. Critic Arthur Sainer considered Ortiz's set "one of the few real lifts of the evening." But he criticized the plodding structure of the play, which he considered a "curious work" that wore out Marlette's ingenuity.[59]

Ray Smith recalled staging problems with Ran Avni. Smith had been in touch with the playwright in Spain and knew, he said, that his directions called for the stage to be lit by firelight in one scene. The lighting designer had used a flickering red light to gain the effect. But Avni objected, saying that the audience would not be able to see the faces.

> I said, "Ran, in this theater, you are no more than thirty feet away. It doesn't matter." But that was where his lack of imagination came in.[60]

Smith had other criticisms of the theater:

Ran was completey disorganized. There was no chain of
command and you never knew where the money came
from or went. You had a budget but we never kept to it....
You didn't have a stable of designers and part of the autonomy was you had to fend for yourself. We were stuck
for a costume designer and took a guy at the last minute
who was atrocious. But Adalberto's sets were really incredible.[61]

The May production was John Van Druten's *I Am a Camera*. Avni
had again advertised in the trade press for directors with play suggestions. Jeff Epstein came to Avni wanting to do the Van Druten
play. Avni felt that the strong anti-Semitic undercurrent in the play
would interest Jewish audiences as a subject, and its success as a musical, also made it an appropriate choice, he felt. The play, based
on the autobiographical *Berlin Stories* by British novelist Christopher
Isherwood, dealt with pre-Nazi Berlin. It was staged in New York
in 1954, followed by the musical version *Cabaret* in 1966 and Bob
Fosse's screen success of 1972. Because of the play's glamorous past,
the JRT production was given major newspaper coverage and was
consequently well attended. It was the first JRT producton to be
reviewed in the *New York Times*, in addition to which a picture was
included. The *New York Post* also ran an advance picture. The *Times*
review, however, was not favorable, although reviewer Thomas Lask
praised Nancy Winter's "skillful, realistic setting." But he criticized
the performances of Bradley Boyer and Denise Lute in the lead roles
of Chris and Sally. "This is one Camera that needs more light," he
summarized.[62] Critic Eva Saks found it "well-acted and superbly
produced, but curiously flat.... The fault is at least in part due to the
play itself, which as the saying goes, loses something in the original English."[63]

The last show of the season, in June, was a comedy by Bonnie Zin-
del called *I Am a Zoo*, which dealt with a psychiatrist and his wife,
their parents, their animals, and their second divorce. While it did
not rate a single review, it proved to be an audience-pleaser, with
fairly good attendance. "Looking back, it was probably an awful
play, but the audience laughed," Avni recalled. "But it was very
hip. Years later Playwrights Horizons would make a whole career
of that—young people, shrinks, flaky writing style."[64]

In all, the 1977-1978 season saw major changes at the JRT, with the advent of a JRT board headed by Alfred Plant, and the onset of fund-raising efforts. Playwrights, actors, directors, designers would come and go, because the JRT was in no position to offer them anything permanent, although the Marlette group did reappear for one production. Betsy Imershein, in handling office and business affairs, introduced, for the first time, a system of reserved seats. Visitng the 92nd Street Y's box office, she picked up pointers in ticket distribution. "Ran and I argued about it, because he hated to turn people away. But I felt we had to clean up our act," Imershein said. "Ran went along with it, but kicking and screaming at first."[65]

The introduction of a reservation system helped allay the problem of Saturday night mayhem. In that early period the Y office staff was handling tickets without a box office window. Because the Y was closed from Friday night to Saturday night (because of the Sabbath), many people would appear Saturday night, seeking tickets. They would compete for space in the office with all other Y office activities. As productions sold out more consistently, there would be thirty or forty people milling about in the small office, vying for ten tickets. Gradually Imershein and Avni educated the Y office so that they converted the office window facing the lobby into a box office.

It was a season that showed a steady growth for the theater, in terms of attendance and box office receipts. The total amount of receipts, the highest to date, was $11,216, with 4669 attendees.

1978-1979

The following fall, the 1978-1979 season, marked further signs of growth. Betsy Imershein made new demands, as her responsibilities grew. She found herself reading scripts, sitting in on rehearsals, auditions, production meetings, and giving her reactions to Avni. That fall she asked that she be given the title of managing director, that it would give her more authority in dealing with others. It was a hard-won victory, she said:

> I kept filling a vacuum, and I wanted the title. Ran was
> not totally happy with it. Clearly the theater was his baby.
> I knew that. But it was the same problem you're likely
> to have with any founding artistic director. Their energy
> built the theater and they don't let go. But that prevents

the theater from growing, after a certain point.[66]

That fall also saw the launching of a subscription program, at the insistence of Imershein, she said. The initial mail order drive preceding the season brought in 200 charter-member subscribers. The fall programs carried the message: "Act Now! Reservations assigned in order received. Enroll me as a charter subscriber." The six shows of the season were offered for $14 (or four Theater Development Fund vouchers plus $2).

It was also the beginning of Edward Cohen's Writers' Lab. Cohen finally gave a formal title to an acitivity he had been developing gradually for some time. He not only read unsolicited works (eventually there would be over 150 a season), but worked closely with the writers in suggesting cuts and changes. He actively and systematically looked for new work, in order to launch playwrights as well as enrich the theater's repertory.

Sifting through manuscripts, he singled out the most promising and went on to hold staged readings of their work. In 1978-1979, Cohen conducted readings for six new plays, among them Richard Schotter's *Benya the King*, a drama that would become an award-winner and go on to full production at the JRT and later at other theaters. Four of the others would also go on to full production.

The season opened with two short plays by Ernest Joselovitz, a contemporary Jewish writer "with some real credits;"[67] *Sammi*, a curtain-raiser that had been published by Samuel French, and *Triptych*, a new play. Joselovitz, had already received recognition for his *Hagar's Children*, which had been produced at the Public Theater. But his two one-acters were not liked by the critics, who found them too wordy. The shorter play deals with an elderly widower who reflects on his wasted life. The second one focusses on a family reunion at a Passover seder in a middle-class Los Angeles suburb.

Avni himself recalled that the plays were depressing and admired the production mainly for the sets of Adalberto Ortiz, which he considered ingenious and consistent with Ortiz's earlier work at the JRT. "The way he switched the sets from one play to another was incredible."[68]

Betsy Imershein remembered an intense experience centered around *Triptych*, in which she and Avni jointly hosted a real *seder* (a Passover feast) for the cast:

We did an abbreviated *seder* with the whole cast, so there would be a shared kind of experience of what the *seder* meant. Some of the actors weren't even Jewish and, for those who were, there were mixed feelings about what the *seder* had been in their lives. That experience reinforced my feeling that I was glad I was involved in theater that was Jewish.[69]

The *Soho News* considered the acting inadequate, the characterization shallow, and the language over-blown.[70] The *New York Theater Review* agreed, in essence, but did praise the acting of Rosalind Harris.[71] Arthur Sainer was somewhat kinder to the perferomers, finding Jay Bonnell "a sympathetic if somewhat awkward Sammi" and added that "Ms. Harris, a classic East European beauty, exhibits a refreshing strength that gives some backbone to a generally flabby evening."[72]

The December play, which came to the JRT by way of an agent, was, Avni said, "a big deal."[73] It involved a well-recognized playwright, Mark Medoff, who had already written the successful *When You Comin' Back, Red Ryder?*, established director J. Rannelli, and award-winning actor Paul Hecht. The play, *The Halloween Bandit*, described as a comedy of menace, concerns a man who invades the apartment of a glamorous television actress on Halloween. The bandit, and the actress's husband, both of Jewish background, have masked their true identities, striving to be part of the Protestant mainstream.

Despite such promising beginnings, the production was plagued with problems. To begin, Paul Hecht became deathly ill just as the play was to open. The opening was postponed a week, therefore, and Hecht was replaced by actor Joel Brooks—"a terrible, difficult, tempermental person," Avni recalled. Because of the spats and mounting tensions that last week, Don Geller threatened to close the show, but was persuaded not to do so. Actors became more testy and demanding, and one performer, Jeanne Ruskin, demanded that the company buy her the necessary tights and leotards for a "nude scene." Avni ordered Imershein (who was co-producing the show with him) to take care of it. "I'm not running to Mays on 14th Street in the middle of the night, in the rain, to get the actress underwear," she said, "unless you come with me."[74] Avni felt he was so deeply involved in the play that he had to see it through, whatever the demands. He complied. But he began to feel that the play—and his very theater—was headed for disaster.

When Gussow's review finally appeared, it was heavily critical, mostly hitting the play itself:

> At his best, Mr. Medoff is an American cousin of Harold Pinter—writing chilling comedies of menace...Unfortunately, this time the premise is shaky and the script borders on self-parody....The play asks questions when it should supply answers, labels when it should demonstrate, recalls when it should dramatize.[75]

The JRT's next production was presented in January and was directed by Edward Cohen. Cohen, who had had some success the previous season with *The Cold Wind and the Warm*, was eager to diect again. He suggested *Unlikely Heroes*, Larry Arrick's adaptation of several Philip Roth short stories, which had played on Broadway in 1970. Cohen suspected that the effort had not succeeded at that time because it was not true to the Jewish spirit of the Roth stories. Cohen cast and directed the show with that in mind, and the JRT production was a success, well received by the audiences. The three short plays—*Defender of the Faith, Epstein*, and *The Fanatic*—all deal with different aspects of contemporary Jewish life, and, Cohen felt, attracted a new, younger audience to the JRT, bringing in "busloads from Long Island."[76]

Betsy Imershein, as producer, saw the show as one of the highlights of her JRT tenure:

> It was very Jewish, and it felt good presenting the show because it really had moral fiber and character. It provoked a lot of different things in the actors who worked on these shows. Ed Cohen had to come to some terms with his Jewishness, as I recalled him saying. And it made people think in a provocative way in a Jewish context.
> I liked being part of that.[77]

The *Village Voice* was critical of the plays, but praised Cohen's production. Arthur Sainer wrote that Arrick could not write plays and that the one-acters were "crawling with undigested bits of narration." But, he added, "In Edward Cohen's moving production of the Roth plays...there are quite credible performances to be seen."[78]

The theater's March show was John Galsworthy's *Loyalties*. Patricia Lawler, who had been part of Don Marlette's group, serving as stage manager for some of his plays, had long wanted to direct a show for Avni. She had been looking for a play that had not been performed frequently, and a friend suggested the Galsworthy drama. The Galsworthy play depicted anti-Semitism in upper middle-class British society after World War I. Lawler liked the even-handed way the play dealt with its issues, and asked to direct it. Avni, after seeing a show she was diecting New Jersey, agreed. But he had other reasons as well:

> I figured she had the script, she had access to good set
> pieces, Don Marlette would help her, the play was real-
> ly a nice play and should have been done by us, so I said
> "What the hell, let's do it."[79]

The play had a cast of eighteen, which included Don Marlette and Avni himself in the role of an Italian wine merchant. "I started as an Italian, but ended up as just a foreigner, because my accent wasn't quite Italian," Avni recalled. "But it was good to be acting again."[80]

The Galsworthy play attracted the attention of the *New York Times*, enough so that a reporter wrote a full feature piece before the show opened, dwelling on the background of the JRT and Avni, and on Lawler's preparation of the show. It was the first such coverage from the newspaper. Avni remembered the experience ecstatically:

> There was a cast party at a Village restaurant on Thurs-
> day night (March 15) and I remember buying the Friday
> paper that night and taking it to the restaurant. I felt like
> I was in seventh heaven! it was the happiest day of my
> life.[81]

Though the *New York Times* did not go on to review the show, the feature story gave the production a great impetus, in terms of ticket sales, and it became a hit. Other New York dailies also ran brief advance notices of the show, but only the Jewish press and the *New York Theater Review* reviewed it. The *Jewish Week-American Examiner* praised the show's performances and direction but was critical of the play itself, insisting that Galsworthy had little knowledge of Jews. As to the British characters:

> Galsworthy clearly understands them and believes they
> have basic decency.... The play is a rather upsetting

reminder that the world has grown considerably more
threatening to Jews.[82]

The spring production was Irwin Shaw's 1939 comic melodrama
The Gentle People, directed by Avni. The play, described by the
author as "A Brooklyn Fable," is about two elderly friends, a Jew
and Greek, who escape from the women in their lives by fishing in
an old boat off Coney Island. Their dream is to buy a larger boat and
go to Cuba to catch swordfish.

Avni's production featured several JRT regulars: Alice Spivak,
Michael Mantel, Gerry Lou (in private life Gerry Lou Silverman and
later a board member of JRT) and proved to be an audience pleaser.
But critics were less supportive. Though the show had good advance
notice in New York papers, only one small New York paper reviewed
the show—*Wisdom's Child*. And that paper gave the play a mixed
review, saying that the play itself, a parable about fascism, was as
fresh as ever, but that the production lacked dynamism. The two lead
actors—Michael Marcus and Robert Coe—did not match the performances of the original Group Theatre production, but there were
good supporting performances from Alice Spivak, Michael Mantel, John Del Regno, and Mark Weston.[83]

The season closed in June with Clifford Odet's *Rocket to the Moon*,
bringing back the Don Marlette group. Marlette was the director,
with Ray Smith as assistant director, Adalberto Ortiz the set designer,
and Patricia Lawler an assistant to the director.

"Don wanted to do the play," Avni recalled, "and, though it did
not have a Jewish theme, it was obvious that it was about Jewish people."[84] Although the play was not reviewed by major papers, it was,
as Avni recalled, a mild success.

In all, 1978-1979 was a season of progress. For the first time, the
major New York newspaper had taken notice of the theater. Also,
ticket subscriptions were launched, with 200 subscribers that first
season, giving a new stability to the theater. And, though actors were
still not paid, as permitted under the theater's continuing showcase
contract, they did get carfare that season, one dollar a show. Box
office receipts jumped to $16,000, $5,000 above the previous year,
with all the money going directly back to the Y, and the Y, in turn,
paying JRT expenses as needed. And finally, said Miss Imershein,
Don Geller became more cooperative:

Once he saw the theater becoming something and getting good reviews, putting him on the map, he started being more supportive, not just going along with it.[85]

1979-1980

The following season saw a major change. The theater moved from
its Equity showcase contract to a non-profit theater code, which required that the actors be paid. Over the next few years the JRT would
maintain that arrangement with Actors Equity, moving from Tier
One through to Tier Three, with increases in actors' salaries accord-
ingly. But in the 1979-1980 season, the theater was on Tier One and
actors were paid $60 per show, including rehearsals. As to further
changes: tickets had jumped to $4, and the productions began to run
four weeks, with four performances a week. The JRT continued to
attract group attendance, with various social groups from Long Island and Brooklyn synagogues, for example, buying blocks of tickets
for JRT shows.

The season opened with Hungarian Ferenc Molnar's drama *Liliom*,
directed by Edward Cohen. Anvi questioned the Jewishness of the
play, but Cohen, who wanted to direct it, pointed out that the play
dealt with Jewish people in high places in pre-war European society. Moreover, the playwright himself was Jewish. They decided to
go with it. It turned out to be, according to Avni, "a certified bomb—a
bad production with a poor actor [Peter Alzado] in the lead."[86]

Critic Richard F. Shepard of the *New York Times* came to see the
show, and, as he walked into the theater, he said, "This is one of
my favorite plays." "Right away you knew you were in trouble!"
said Avni.[87] He was right. Shepard dismissed the production by
saying:

> The magic that made this play into a sturdy, long-lived
> piece of theater does not come through in this produc-
> tion....Molnar was Hungarian and one suspects that his
> play...could use a dash of paprika.[88]

Both Shepard and Avni himself felt that the play, with its fragile
charm, called for the most careful casting, and, lacking that, the
production failed.

The second show, *Benya the King*, in contrast, delighted audiences,
enjoying an extended run of twenty performances in December and

January. The Schotter play, based on Isaac Babel's *Tales of Odessa*, had had a successful staged reading the previous season at the JRT and was expected to do well. Cohen, who had worked closely with Schotter throughout the play's development, considered him a fine and careful craftsman.

Directed by Roger Hendrick Simon, the play, though not a musical, brought live music to the theater for the first time and helped to create a fantasy setting. *Benya* is a kind of fairy tale about a scrapman's son who turns to crime and becomes a Robin Hood. It is set in Odessa, where Jews lived a much more cosmopolitan life than elsewhere in eastern Europe, speaking Russian rather than Yiddish, and the play deals with changing Jewish values.

The play was well publicized, with advance announcements in the *Times, Daily News, Post*, and *Variety*. And the *Post*, though not the others, reviewed the show. Clive Barnes, wrote that "a smidgen of cynicism has replaced a large pinch of sentimentality," and "the performances were carefully stylized and often stylish."[89] The paper at Queens College (where Schotter teaches) was, understandably, enthusiastic:

> The language is vibrant, colorful and exquisite in its metaphors. While ingenious and often hilarious staging techniques are liberally used to exemplify much of the play's content...Schotter's skillfully depictive lines dismiss the need for further physical staging.[90]

The Jewish press was less florid:

> *Benya the King* is an interesting and amusing script that takes a fresh look at a little-known aspect of Russian-Jewish life. The JRT is doing a service in encouraging Jewish playwrights by giving their works competent productions.[91]

Burton Feinberg felt that the performances were strong, but the play did not come off:

> A murder early in the story dispels the air of fantasy which is so crucial to the play. The pace is slow (although some lively music provides a partial cure) and the ending is abrupt, leaving the viewer somewhat dissatisfied.[92]

At the end of January, Thornton Widler's *The Matchmaker* was produced. Avni was somewhat reluctant because the Jewish connections were dubious. But Don Marlette, who had directed three previous JRT shows, was eager to direct it. He brought in Ray Smith and Patricia Lawler again to help, along with several HB students/actors.

Wilder's farce had, in fact, a connection to the Jewish theme, although a tenuous one: its central character was a matchmaker, a familiar type in Yiddish theater, and her name, Dolly Levi, was Jewish, although acquired by marriage. The one presumably Jewish character, her husband, had died long ago.

Despite Wilder's prestigious reputation, the play was not reviewed nor well attended. Perhaps both critics and audiences tended to ignore the show because it did not seem to be JRT fare, although it is hard to evaluate the New York critic's reasons for by-passing a show.

The spring production, however, made up for *The Matchmaker*. It was *Green Fields* by Peretz Hirshbein, a tale of a Russian-Jewish family at the turn of the century. It was actress Lynn Polan's first directing assignment at the JRT, and she was deeply grateful for the opportunity:

> Ran had seen me direct a one-act play at the Counterpoint
> Theatre Company and he liked it enough to ask me to
> direct. That's pretty risky for an artistic director, because,
> if he hires a lousy director, the whole thing goes down
> the tubes. I was grateful for his confidence in me.[93]

Originally plans were to present *Dark at the Top of the Stairs*, but, after the JRT had already scheduled it, the Roundabout Theater announced its plans to produce the play, and Avni hurriedly began to search for a replacement. Avni and Polan, in their recollections, each take credit for finding *Green Fields*. The play was the Peretz Hirshbein classic about humble country Jews in Russia at the turn of the century. It was in the collection of Jewish plays translated by Queens College professor Joseph Landis which the JRT had drawn upon earlier. Said Polan:

> It was a wonderful, wise choice for me as a beginning
> director, because it was about the 1890s in Poland, a play
> about a family, about parents and children and growing
> up and falling in love and being young and trying to find
> out what the world was about—things I really under-
> stood.[94]

Alfred Plant was not impressed with the choice when Avni gave him the play to read. "Fred said, 'I wouldn't cross town to see this play, but I guess it's nice.' It turned out to be our first *New York Times* rave. It was a hit of the magnitude we had not seen before."[95]

But Lynn Polan had substantial problems with the production, beyond the usual JRT difficulties caused by a limited budget and skeleton staff:

> We were always holding on by our fingertips to get technical things done. It was hard to find good people with such a low budget.... We had a student designer (Cecilia Gilchriest) who didn't know what she was doing, although she appeared to in the beginning. We had to bring in Jeffrey Schneider. And we also lost an actress, Fanchon Miller, who was hurt in an auto accident. Alice Spivak came in at the last minute.[96]

Alive Spivak recalled:

> I got the call, I believe, Wednesday, the day before opening, and agreed to do it. I asked them to cancel the Thursday night opening, which was an organizational problem for Ran, but he did it, and we opened Saturday. I did it off the book.[97]

There was a special excitement and special audience involvement, Spivak said:

> Saturday night they announced to the audience that I had just come in and might call for lines. The audience loved being in on it. But, by the second week, I no longer called for lines.... It was a lovely experience and possibly good that I came in late. It shook up the cast.... The cast was uneven, but I didn't have time to sit around and think about it.[98]

For Jeffrey Schneider, it was the beginning of a long association with JRT, but it was a rocky initiation:

> I was the first designer who said "I am not a carpenter, I am a designer. You are going to have to hire somebody to build it." Ran had never heard that before. As a result he fired me. Lynn didn't have enough clout or didn't really stand up for me. But after someone else built a set that was sort of a disaster, I was called back. Then Ran offered me the full fee, and the next season Ran met all my demands.[99]

Reviewers were as responsive to the play as audiences. "Who would have expected that one of the season's most delightful performances would be an off-off-Broadway production of a 70-year-old play translated from the Yiddish?" *Hadassah Magazine* exclaimed.[100] And Richard F. Shepard of the *New York Times* exulted, using such terms as "delicious scenes" and saying that it was difficult to single out stars from the admirable cast: "It is a tribute to its endearing qualities that it not only stands up, even blossoms, after all these years, but does so in English translation."[101]

Green Fields was also Betsy Imershein's farewell production, and, in terms of its success, she left on a high note. But leave she did. Her departure was brought on by a number of frustrations with the Y, with Geller, and with Avni. As managing director, she found her power restricted. In applying for a grant, for example:

> I spent many months in the Foundation Library research-
> ing places where we could apply for funding, and, after
> all this work Don Geller said, "I don't want you to do
> it." He wanted it all to be through him; he was very con-
> trolling.[102]

Imershein felt that there were innumerable other problems with having the theater housed at the Y—the disinterest, inefficiency and sometimes downright dishonesty of the Y staffers—all of which blocked the theater's operation. She had often urged Avni to move the theater, but he was adamant about remaining.

> I appreciated the need of the theater beginning there, but
> I felt remaining there was holding the theater back. But
> Ran wouldn't leave.[103]

The April 1980 production was Neil Simon's *Come Blow Your Horn*, directed by Avni himself. Avni recalled that there were difficulties getting the rights to the play:

> I asked and was refused and then wrote Simon, telling
> him that our Jewish theater was going to highlight aspects
> of the play neglected before. And, all of a sudden, we got
> the rights.[104]

The comedy takes place in the 1960s and focusses on two Jewish bachelor brothers living on New York's upper East Side and trying to break free of their parents. While the production was not reviewed by any major paper, smaller area papers praised the performances and the production.

The JRT's final production of the season was *36*, an original comedy written by Norman Lessing. Avni recalled:

> This guy, a former TV writer, sent me this play from
> California. He said a big-name director (I think it was
> Sidney Lumet) was dying to do his play. I liked the play
> and agreed to do it. But later we found out that the director
> wasn't available. We didn't know what to do, and, at that
> point, it was dropped.[105]

But Lessing did not give up so easily, Avni said:

> All of a sudden Lessing calls and says he has a TV direc-
> tor, Marc Daniels, who had directed *Alice* and *Hogan's
> Heroes*, but was originally in theater. Sure enough,
> Daniels came.[106]

Daniels was appalled at the sight of the theater space, Avni said. "He had had an open heart operation, and I thought he was going to have a heart attack."[107] But they chatted, with Avni telling Daniels about the Y's swimming pool, and Daniel's doubts faded with the prospect of a daily swim. Moreover, he liked the play. At that point in the theater's history, actors were paid $60 a production, and Daniels was given the same amount. Daniels' agent joked about the pay, asking whether Avni meant $60 an hour or a day. In effect, Daniels freely contributed his high-priced talents—and also contributed some $2000, to provide for an extended run, with more advertising. The play had its regular 16-performance run in June and was extended into the summer for an additional thirty performances, bringing in a total gate (regular and extended run combined) of almost $20,000.

The comedy is based on the legend that there are thirty-six humble men in every generation who are so saintly that God saves the world for their sake. Three Hasidic Jews visit Cincinnati to find the last of the saints—a humble electrician, as it turns out. The comedy emerges from the conflict between blind faith and modern skepticism. Avni acknowledged that Daniels had trouble with the ending but summarized the production as a "charming, lovely piece of theater" that subscribers talked about for years after.[108] Shepard saw the play as lightweight but entertaining, closing with the comment that "there are worse ways to spend time on a hot night."[109]

In all, as the JRT moved into the 1980s, the theater saw considerable changes. The 1979-1980 season brought in box office receipts of $32,000, double the previous year. Subscriptions had climbed to about 360 by the beginning of the season. *Benya* enjoyed the largest attendance to date, with a total attendance of 2231, and *Green Fields*, though with a lesser attendance of 1697, was a solid critical and popular hit. JRT productions had moved into longer runs, based on a new Equity contract, and its actors were at last being paid for their work. Although the theater still worked with a skeleton staff, with only Avni full-time and salaried (Imershein having left that season), Avni had built up a stable of theater people. Such people as directors Don Marlette and Lynn Polan, actors Michael Mantel and Alice Spivak, and set designers Adalberto Ortiz and Jeffrey Scheider would return frequently. And Edward Cohen, with his Writers' lab, was attracting new young playwrights and working with them on scripts, with a total of eight scripts developed during the 1979-80 season. Major newspapers had become aware of the JRT and had given some of its shows excellent reviews. And, above all, the theater was steadily building a loyal audience, with theatergoers who returned again and again.

[1]Ran Avni, interview, New York City, 22 July 1985.

[2]Ibid.

[3]"East and West the Twain Meet," *Village Voice*, 6 October 1975.

[4]"A Night in May," *Backstage*, 10 October 1975.

[5]"War Drama," *Hadassah Magazine*, November 1975.

[6]Michael Mantel, interview, New York City, 28 May 1985.

[7]Avni, interview, 22 July 1985.

[8]Ibid.

[9]Ibid.

[10]Elenore Lester, "Yiddish repertory offers two plays on forgotten Jews," *The Jewish Week-American Examiner*, 30 November-6 December 1975.

[11]The fact is that in the past many an actor headed up his own company. And one can cite, in Yiddish theater, such actor/directors as Maurice Schwartz and Jacob Ben Ami. But, generally, in today's times, theaters are not run by actors.

[12]Hannah Grad Goodman, "A Mythical Country?" *Hadassah Magazine*, April 1976.

[13]Valerie Owen, *"Andora* Wins Praise," *East Side (New York) Courier*, 12 February 1976, p. 4.

[14]Avni, interview, 6 June 1985.

[15]The Jewish Court was an informal self-imposed institution that existed outside the U.S. judicial system, not unlike rabbinic courts in earlier times. It was established on the Lower East Side over sixty years ago when Jewish immigrants streamed into the city. The aim was to carry out justice simply, in accordance with Jewish law and customs, common sense and humanity. It was understood that all parties concerned would accept the determination of the judges, who were often uptown Jewish lawyers and judges giving their expertise freely after working hours. In fact, Justice Louis Brandeis was among the volunteers.

[16]Alice Spivak, interview, New York City, 31 May 1985.

[17]Ibid.

[18]Avni, interview, 6 June 1985. Avni was actually ahead of his time, because in 1985 the musical *The Mystery of Edwin Drood* resorted to just that "gimmick," to the delight of Broadway audiences.

[19]*Jewish Daily Forward*, May 1976.

[20]Nancy Kelton, "Sketches Lack Conflict," *East Side Courier*, 6 May 1976.

[21]*Hadassah Magazine*, "Sight and Sound," June 1976.

[22]Avni, interview, 16 July 1985.

[23]Ibid.

[24]Sy Syna, "Review," *Wisdom's Child*, 13 September 1976.

[25]Shelly Uva, "Flaws Dent Chayevsky play," *Eastside Courier*, 9 September 1976.

[26]Elenore Lester, "Chayevsky play revived at 14th st. Y; ran 2 years on Broadway 20 years ago," *The Jewish Week-American Examiner*, 19-25 September 1976.

[27]Avni, interview, 16 July 1985.

[28]*Show Business*, 11 November 1976.

[29]The fictional Cafe Crown is based on the one-time Cafe Royal at Second Avenue and 12th Street.

[30]Avni, interview, 16 July 1985.

[31]Ernest Leogrande, "No Crown this Round," *New York Daily News*, 4 December 1976.

[32]Fred Berliner, "This Week," *Show Business*, 16 December 1976.

[33]Jeannie Schulman, "Cafe Crown," *Back Stage*, 14 January 1977.

[34]Stefan Schnabel, telephone interview, Rowayton, Connecticut, 15 October 1985.

[35]Ibid.

[36]Arthur Sainer, "Condemned To Think, Feel and Screw," *Village Voice*, 28 March 1977.

[37]Schnabel, interview, 15 October 1985.

[38]Avni, interview, 16 July 1985.

[39]Avni, interview, 28 July 1985.

[40]Ray Smith, interview, New York City, 31 May 1985.

[41]Ibid.

[42]Mark Spergel, interview, New York City, 29 May 1985.

[43]Smith, interview, 31 May 1985.

[44]Linda Stein, "Deft 'Ivanov' Done," *Chelsea Clinton News*, 23 June 1977.

[45]Elenore Lester, "Chekhov owes revival to Jewish angle," *Jewish Week-American Examiner*, 12 June 1977.

[46]Debbi Wasserman, "The Cold Wind and the Warm," *New York Theatre Review*, January 1978.

[47]Holly Hill, "Dancing in New York City," *New York Theatre Review*, February 1978.

[48]Hannah Grad Goodman, "New York Bachelors," *Hadassah Magazine*, February 1978.

[49]Betsy Imershein, interview, New York City, 13 June 1985.

[50]Ibid.

[51]Alfred Plant, interview, New York City, 18 October 1984.

[52]Clive Barnes, "Stage: Modern 'Venice,'" *New York Times*, 5 March 1973.

[53]Avni, interview, 28 July 1986.

[54]Ibid.

[55]John Bush Jones, "The Merchant of Venice," *New York Theatre Review*, April 1978.

[56]Barbara Garson, "Straight Bard," *Village Voice*, 20 February 1978.

[57]Avni, who had studied accordion from the age of twelve, had performed a one-man show (playing, singing and telling jokes) for a number of years. He finally abandoned the show when he turned to the JRT full-time, but he did play the accordion in a number of JRT shows.

[58]Smith, interview, 31 May 1984.

[59]Arthur Sainer, "A Wan War at the Y," *Village Voice*, 3 April 1978.

[60]Smith, interview, 31 May 1985.

[61]Ibid.

[62]Thomas Lask, "Stage: Ageless," *New York Times*, 14 May 1978.

[63]Eva Saks, "I Am a Camera," *Casting Call*, 24-30 May 1978.

[64]Avni, interview, 16 July 1985.

[65]Imershein, interview, 13 June 1985.

[66]Ibid.

[67]Avni, interview, 16 July 1985.

[68]Ibid.

[69]Imershein, interview, 13 June 1985.

[70]*Soho News*, 5-11 October 1978.

[71]Alvin Klein, "Sammi and Triptych," *New York Theatre Review*, November 1978.

[72]Arthur Sainer, "What Makes Sammi Glum," *Village Voice*, 9 October 1978.

[73]Avni, interview, 16 July 1985.

[74]Ibid.

[75]Mel Gussow, "Stage: 'Halloween Bandit'—A Comedy of Menace," *New York Times*, 19 December 1978.

[76]Rob Edelman, "The Cultural Scene," *Jewish Monthly*, June-July 1984.

[77]Imershein, interview, 13 June 1985.

[78]Arthur Sainer, "Two Men's Worlds," *Village Voice*, 5 February 1979.

[79] Avni, interview, 22 July 1985.

[80]Ibid.

[81]Ibid.

[82]"British bigotry to be dissected at Midtown Y," *Jewish Week-American Examiner*, 11 March 1979.

[83]"The Gentle People," *Wisdom's Child*, 14-20 May 1979.

[84]Avni, interview, 19 July 1985.

[85]Imershein, interview, 13 June 1985.

[86]Avni, interview, 22 July 1985.

[87]Ibid.

[88]Richard F. Shepard, "Stage: Jewish Repertory Revives Molnar's 'Liliom,'" *New York Times*, 2 November 1979.

[89]Clive Barnes, " 'Benya the King' by Jewish Repertory," *New York Post*, 10 January 1980.

[90]Penni-Ellen Bergholz, "Schotter's Inspiration," *Queens College*, 17 December 1978.

[91]Goodman, "Tales of Odessa," *Hadassah Magazine*, March 1980.

[92]Burton Feinberg, "Jewish Robin Hood Gives Hope," *Jewish World*, 11 January 1980.

[93]Lynn Polan, interview, New York City, 5 April 1985.

[94]Ibid.

[95]Avni, interview, 22 July 1985.

[96]Polan, interview, 5 April 1985.

[97]Alice Spivak, interview, 31 May 1985.

[98]Ibid.

[99]Jeffrey Schneider, interview, New York City, 10 June 1985.

[100]"Country Jews," *Hadassah Magazine*, May 1980.

[101]Richard F. Shepard, " 'Green Fields' produced by Jewish Repertory," *New York Times*, 23 March 1980.

[102]Imershein, interview, 13 June 1985.

[103]Ibid.

[104]Avni, interview, 22 July 1985.

[105]Ibid.

[106]Ibid.

[107]Ibid.

[108]Ibid.

[109]Richard F. Shepard, "Theater: Jewish Repertory Stages '36,'" *New York Times*, 27 June 1980.

1. *above*
GOD OF VENGEANCE
October 1974—left to right, Lillian Lux,
Avner Regev, Martha Schlamme.
Photo by H. Katz.

2. *middle*
LADY OF THE CASTLE
April 1975—left to right, Elise Hunt,
Avner Regev, and Lynn Polan.
Photo by Barbara Gingold.

3. *below*
THE CLOSING OF MENDEL'S CAFE
November 1975—left to right,
Avner Regev and Lynn Polan.

4. *above*
EAST SIDE JUSTICE
June 1976—left to right,
Alice Spivak and Lynn Polan.

5. *middle*
CAFE CROWN
December 1976—left to right,
Glen Alterman, Gerry Lou, Jeffrey
Rodman, Allen Swift, Barbara
Marchant, Aaron Altman.

6. *below*
THE CONDEMNED OF ALTONA
February 1977—left to right standing,
Stefan Schnabel, Gregory Chase;
seated, Chris Weatherhead.

7. *above left*
IVANOV
June 1977—left to right, James
Goodwin Rice and Rosalind Greer.
Photo by Stanley Lawler.

8. *above right*
DANCING IN NEW YORK CITY
December 1977—left to right,
Carol Rosenfeld and Herb Duncan.
Photo by Maureen Brierton.

9. *middle*
I AM A CAMERA
May 1978—left to right,
Bradley Boyer and Denise Lute.

10. *below*
ANNA KLEIBER
March 1978—left to right,
Jennifer Sternberg and Jonas McCord.

11. *top*
TRIPTYCH
October 1978—left to right,
Rosalind Harris and Felicity Adler.

12. *middle*
HALLOWEEN BANDIT
December 1978—left to right,
Jeanne Ruskin and Joel Brooks.

13. *bottom*
LOYALTIES
March 1979—left to right, Stanley Kahn,
Bruce Kent, Don Marlette.

14. *top*
GENTLE PEOPLE
May 1979—left to right,
Denise Lute and John Del Regno.

15. *middle*
LILIOM
October 1979—left to right,
Michael Mantel and Peter Alzado.
Photo by Robert Grodman.

16. *bottom*
GREEN FIELDS
March 1980—left to right,
Fanchon Miller and Alan Brandt.

17. *top*
INCIDENT AT VICHY
May 1981—left to right,
Ran Avni and playwright Arthur Miller.
Photo by Trish Jenkins.

18. *middle left*
INCIDENT AT VICHY
May 1981—left to right,
William Brenner and Robin Chadwick.

19. *middle right*
ELEPHANTS
December 1981—left to right,
Marilyn Chris and Lee Wallace.

20. *bottom*
PANTAGLEIZE
April 1982—left to right, Ellen Barber and
Joel Bernstein. Photo by Ann Blackstock.

21. *top*
Staged reading, December 1982—
left to right, Colleen Dewhurst,
Ran Avni, Judd Hirsch.
Photo by Ricki Rosen.

22. *middle*
TAKING STEAM
April 1983—left to right,
Frank Nastasi, Herb Duncan,
Jack Aaron, Harvey Pierce (rear),
Maurice Sterman, Felix Fibich
(rear), Herman Arbeit.
Photo by Adam Newman.

23. *bottom*
MY HEART IS IN THE EAST
June 1983—left to right,
John Towey and Susan Victor.
Photo by Adam Newman.

24. *top*
UP FROM PARADISE
October 1983—left to right,
musical director Michael Ward,
Austin Pendleton, Walter Bobbie,
Alice Playten, playwright Arthur
Miller, stage manager G. Franklin
Heller, Len Cariou, Paul Ukena, Jr.,
director Ran Avni, Lonny Price.
Photo by Inge Morath.

25. *center*
UP FROM PARADISE
October 1983—left to right,
Avery Tracht, Richard Frisch,
Austin Pendelton, Len Cariou.
Photo by Inge Morath.

26. *right*
GIFTED CHILDREN
December 1983—left to right, Ben
Siegler, Dinah Manoff and Zohra
Lampert. Photo by Adam Newman.

27. *above*
THE HOMECOMING
February 1984—left to right,
Howard Sherman, Charles Randall,
William McNulty, Cheryl McFadden,
Mark Arnott, Joe Silver.
Photo by John Cole.

28. *middle*
THE HOMECOMING
February 1984—left to right,
Joe Silver and Charles Randall.
Photo by John Cole.

29. *below*
KUNI-LEML
June 1984—left to right, first row:
master electrician Linda Burns, stage
manager Gay Smerek, Stuart Zagnit,
Scott Wentworth, Barbara McCulloh.
Second row: Gene Varrone, Daniel
Marcus, Susan Victor, director Ran
Avni, Mark Zeller, musical director
Haila Strauss, and Jack Savage.
Photo by Adam Newman.

30. *top*
KUNI-LEML
June 1984—left to right,
Susan Victor and Stuart Zagnit.
Photo by Adam Newman.

31. *middle*
SHLEMIEL THE FIRST
October 1984—left to right,
Isaac Bashevis Singer and Ran Avni.
Photo by Barbara Marlin.

32. *right*
CITY BOY
February 1985—seated left to right:
DeLane Matthews, Max Cantor.
Standing: Scott Miller.
Photo by Carol Rosegg.

33. CROSSING DELANCEY
May 1985—left to right,
Melanie Mayron and Sylvia Kauders.
Photo by Adam Newman.

34. PEARLS
July 1985—left to right,
Daniel Neiden and Rosalind Elias.

35. RAN AVNI
Artistic Director of the Jewish Repertory Theatre. Photo by Carol Rosegg.

4

Moving Into The Eighties

1980-1981

By 1980, the Jewish Repertory Theatre could well boast of a growing reputation. As the new decade began, additional policy changes were implemented. When the 1980-1981 season opened on October 15, with Gertrude Berg's *Me and Molly*, the JRT began to offer five performances a week—Wednesday, Thursday, Saturday nights, and two performances on Sunday. Subscriptions at that point had doubled from the previous year to about 680. Ticket prices, which had been edging up gradually each year, increased to $5 and $6 that season. Ticket acquisition was also made more stringent. Reservations made on performance day, for example, were held only until a half hour before curtain, so that the theater did not lose money holding tickets that were never picked up.

It was the second year of the company's Non-Profit Theater Tier One contract with Equity, and actors, under the contract, were paid $60 for an entire show, with no extra money for rehearsals. Avni decided to pay others involved in the show in the same way. "It was my brilliant idea to give everybody the same amount, just like a kibbutz," he said.[1]

The season's opener was adapted and directed by Cohen. "I had a lot of confidence in Ed, and right after he did *Liliom* last year, we talked about a show this year, and he said he had a good idea."[2] Cohen's "good idea" was an adaptation of Gertrude Berg's *Me and Molly*, which had played Broadway in 1948. The comedy, which depicts the life of a Bronx Jewish family, was originally a radio series called "The Rise of the Goldbergs" and ran, with few lapses, from 1929 to 1945, and later enjoyed one season on television. Cohen went back to the original Broadway play, cutting and rewriting for a new, more streamlined version. The production featured Julie Garfield, John Garfield's daughter, in the title role. Although she was younger and more attractive than the fabled Molly Goldberg, she played the part convincingly. "It was a courageous decision to play the part of an older woman, but it worked."[3]

The play proved highly popular with the JRT audiences and critics found it amiable. Richard F. Shepard wrote that it was a "welcome comic interval and a fitting opener for the company's seventh season."[4]

The December offering was a revival of the John Howard Lawson play *Success Story*, which was produced initially in 1932 by the Group Theatre. Lawson, writing in the 1920s and 1930s, typified the radical playwrights of that era, and in fact went on in 1947 to become one of the "Hollywood Ten," vilified and ostracized for his left-wing connections.

Success Story does indeed make a strong political statement, and the play's effectiveness is in fact restricted by its polemics. The story deals with a young radical who disavows his youthful views and goes on to be obsessed by the drive for money and power. The play brought together several JRT alumni: Lynn Polan as director, Michael Albert Mantel as actor, and Jeffrey Schneider as set designer.

Mantel, playing the lead, saw *Success Story* as one turning point in his career, because "I received tremendous notices, including a picture in the *Times*, and an agent saw the play and later contacted me for work."[5] Mantel, who had studied with Lynn Polan at HB Studio, found himself responding easily to her direction and thought she was probably the best director he had ever worked with:

> She's comfortable enough to allow her actors to do their work. Then, when the story gets told, she starts slowly tinkering with it and gets profoundly original staging. The role of the director is by nature one of nurturing, which I think is easier for a female.[6]

The play also represented a step forward in set design, according to Jeffrey Schneider:

> I made a lot of demands on Ran. We had someone come in to build the show, which was a big step for him, and he ended up doing that all year. He had become aware that it helped the total production.[7]

Avni had such limited funds available (he had to ask Geller for money for each item) that of course he wanted to keep production costs down, and, for that reason, if he could have continued to have set designers build their own sets, he would have done so.

Success Story was a qualified success, with both the critics and the audiences. Avni did receive some hate mail which in effect asked him how he dared to present a Communist play. On the other hand, many spectators were voluble in their approval. Mantel recalls an incident one night:

> It was a melodrama and in the end I got shot on stage. As soon as the shot went off, somebody in the audience yelled, "Oooh, right in the *kishkes*!"[8] It sort of broke the tension.[9]

Richard F. Shepard had strong praise for the production, although he gave qualified praise to the play itself, which he saw as splendid in its first two acts, but dropping to melodrama in the last:

> Under the direction of Lynn Polan, the play strongly puts across the moral preachments of the perils of capitalism that inspired the author. Michael Albert Mantel, as the misbegotten hero, is marvelously human, yet malevolent.... The cast around him contribute to making this vignette of Depression-era life come alive.[10]

The January 1981 play was Harold Pinter's *The Birthday Party*, directed by Anthony McKay. McKay, a busy actor and playwright as well as director, a graduate of Carnegie-Mellon University, was already gaining a reputation in New York theater circles. Avni and McKay were introduced to each other by Gerry Lou Silverman (an actress under the name of Gerry Lou) who had performed at the JRT, was on its board of directors, and was in general an active recruiter. "She was wonderful about getting people together," said McKay of Silverman (who died in August 1985). "She dragged Ran up to see my work at the Ensemble Studio Theater."[11]

Edward Cohen had been urging Avni to consider a Pinter play because he pointed out that Pinter was not only British but also Jewish, and that both backgrounds were reflected in his work. Avni, after library research which revealed to him that some critics found Jewish themes in Pinter, decided to stage *The Birthday Party*. As with all Pinter plays, the plot of *The Birthday Party* is insignificant, the atmosphere all-important. Two thugs appear at a tacky English seaside boarding house, in order to seize and carry off the sole boarder. Characters move through a murky, threatening milieu, uttering banalitites, as in a nightmare. The play deals with the themes of anxiety and isolation and powerlessness—themes which relate, however, not only to the Jewish experience, but to all human experience. Jews cannot claim them exclusively. The play, in my view, reflects only limited Jewish connections, which are based on the presence of one clearly Jewish character and his references to his ethnic background. Such is not true for every Pinter play. Three years later, when Avni staged *The Homecoming*, he chose a Pinter play which could have much more meaning for Jews.

The Birthday Party was the beginning of McKay's ongoing association with Avni. For the next several years he directed one play annually, including another Pinter play and a Chekhov drama. He was happy to identify with the JRT, although he saw its exclusive adherence to Jewish material as restrictive, holding back its chance to explore and grow. But McKay found Avni "a dream of an artistic director, who did not constantly look over your shoulder, which has not been my experience at other theaters."[12] McKay discovered that working at the JRT was "more fun" than, for example, the Ensemble Studio Theatre, where a tighter rein was kept on directors. "Ran did come in at dress rehearsals and make suggestions," he said. "And that was helpful because he does have good instincts—theater savvy."[13] McKay had some difficulties with the Y in terms of rehearsal space, which was available only at the Y's convenience. But it generally worked out, McKay said, because the Y was not busy at night.

He found that the JRT's audiences provided a new experience. "They let you know what they think with their feet. They walked out if they didn't like it."[14] Some viewers, he reported, were puzzled by *The Birthday Party* and departed early in the evening, with one women commenting loudly, "British *mishigas*!"[15] Others felt that the play had nothing to do with Jewishness and was inappropriate for the JRT. But one woman, responding to the banal breakfast dialogue over corn flakes, cried aloud, "Just like home!"[16]

McKay did not find his non-Jewishness a problem in directing the play. Working with a play about *Hasidim*, for example, might have been difficult, but he saw Pinter's work as universal. He felt that he was tuned into, and faithfully conveyed, the play's symbolism, with its themes of guilt and repression. "I am the kind of director who really serves the play, who tries to define what the playwright intended."[17]

In analyzing the play, McKay found that the script, with its minimalist dialogue, was suited to a sparse set and to the small JRT stage. He felt that it was, in all, a good show, though not one calculated to have mass appeal. Critics agreed that the production was well done, but, curiously, none questioned whether the play was appropriate for a so-called Jewish theater. One did question the value of the play itself. John Patterson asked:

> There's no denying that Harold Pinter's "The Birthday Party," as produced by the Jewish Rep Theatre, is a job well done; the question is, "Was the job worth doing at all?"... People used to take Pinter's rejection of story-making as an indication that his vision had a deeper, larger focus. Perhaps he has nothing to say so he lops off the legs of a story every time.[18]

The brief *New York Times* review added little light or more understanding of the play, although Jennifer Dunning praised the performances.[19]

The March production, a play called *Marya*, was noteworthy in the sense that so little can be found in the JRT records concerning the experience. The play was not reviewed, and Avni remembers it only as "a real bomb."[20] The play was a late choice, filling the slot for a previously planned production, and was directed by Patricia Lawler. Avni had doubts about the choice, but Lawler, who had successfully directed *Loyalties* two years earlier, liked the play. The original Isaac Babel story, set in Petrograd in 1920, deals with divorce among Jews. The play was adapted by Christopher Hampton from a translation by Michael Glenny and Harold Shukman. Avni was intrigued mainly because the play had never been done in the United States, but later looked back on the performance as "embarrassingly bad."[21]

The following production, however, more than made up for the shortcomings of *Marya*. It was Arthur Miller's *Incident at Vichy*, directed by Avni himself. The production ran in May and June, and was brought back the following September. It was a financial as well as critical success, in fact, one of the biggest money-makers the company had yet experienced, bringing in a total gate of $16,600. Moreover, it proved to be Miller's favorite production of the widely-performed drama, and he returned three times to see the play. Avni claimed that Miller preferred it to the London production, which had starred Alec Guinness. The play was more successful at the JRT, Avni believed, than in its original 1964 Lincoln Center production, because audiences were much more comfortable seeing it as an outright Jewish issue.

Avni had been thinking for some time about the Miller play and had tried for a year to get permission to stage it. He contacted Samuel French and then Miller's agent, Bridget Aschenberg. At first she refused, saying that Miller was anticipating a major production of the drama. Then suddenly Avni was told that Miller would let him do it, but that he wanted to meet the director. Speaking to Miller on the phone, Avni suggested Miller come to the first reading and talk to the cast. Miller agreed, and Avni arranged for the reading in a Y classroom, because "I didn't want him to see the theater."[22] But Miller, as it turned out, paid little attention to the room, concentrating on the cast and the reading, and speaking to the cast encouragingly. Miller explained that the theme of the play was the gradual discovery of evil in the world.

The one-act ninety-minute drama takes place in the basement of an old police station in Vichy, France, where ten men, suspected of being Jewish, have been rounded up. The conflict of attitudes is revealed as the men, who disappear one at a time, communicate with each other and the Nazi officer in charge. The lead character, an Austrian prince, has no awareness of the long history of anti-Semitism and is gradually educated to its meaning by a Jewish doctor. He grows in awareness, ultimately sacrificing his own life for the doctor. As Richard Shepard summarized: "This is Arthur Miller at his most searching and provocative, peeling the leaves of motivation as though they were coming off an artichoke."[23]

Avni felt that he had assembled a "terrific cast"[24]—seventeen men of all ages. In the leads were Robin Chadwick, a one-time British television star, as the Austrian prince, and William Brenner as the Jewish doctor.

The set, designed by Adalberto Ortiz, pleased Avni very much. He went so far as to say that the concept was brilliant.

> He said that the theater looks like a basement anyhow, and with a tiny window at the top of the set, it will be clear it's below ground. He used the idea of a train sound (because there was a train station nearby), using the sound each time concentration camps were mentioned. You had no idea the trains were going to the camps, but the association was there.[25]

Both audiences and critics responded enthusiastically and deplored the fact that it would have such a short run. Under Avni's direction, said Richard Shepard, it became a "live and real situation."

> Even before the audience is seated, the detainees are filling up the room on stage, faces twisted in perplexity or despair, to the accompaniment of the sounds of trains, those dreaded trains rumored to be carrying Jews to extermination, just outside. As the house lights darken, the play commences with a state of tension already existing and it maintains the pace all the way through.[26]

The show sold out for every performance, and, as a result, Avni brought it back in September under a mini-contract. Under the arrangement with Equity, for the JRT's 99-seat theater, participants were given contracts and paid salaries of $100-plus weekly and the show was allowed to run for three more weeks. In the September production actor/director Anthony McKay replaced Frank Anderson as the German officer, because of Anderson's other commitments.

Reviewing the show in September, the *Soho News* was equally ebullient. The critic said that Miller:

> richly deserves the serious rehearsing that the JRT, for all its cramped space and limited resources, is according him with its revival of *Incident at Vichy*. It reminds us that a playwright who habitually aims for the constellations can sometimes take his audience along. [27]

In all, Avni looked back on the production as one of the best plays he ever directed, and claimed that his audiences continued to talk about the play for years after. Even though his most solid successes have come with the musicals, the Miller play has occupied a special niche in his career—and probably his heart. "Everything about it— the cast, the sets, the sound—was just so right!" [28]

1981-1982

Following the Miller play, the 1981-1982 season continued to be another glorious year for the JRT. The theater moved on to a Tier Two Equity contract, paying its actors $230 per show. Its very next production, *Awake and Sing!*, the 1930s play that brought fame to writer Clifford Odets and the Group Theatre, was a hit. It was the realistic, bittersweet story of a Jewish family in the Bronx, a tale of discontent and struggle.

Avni originally applied for the Odets play *Paradise Lost* but did not get permission from the agent, Selma Lutinger, of Brandt & Brandt, who handled the Odets estate. The play had not been done in New York for many years, and they were probably holding out for a major New York production, Avni believed. He then requested permission for *Awake and Sing!*, which was approved informally, as he understood it. Avni went ahead, announcing the production, selecting Lynn Polan as director, and proceeding to cast. He then received a call from the furious agent, who said, "Under no circumstances are you doing it. The Odets estate never give people permission." Clearly, there had been a misunderstanding: Avni believed he had been given permission while the agent saw it merely as an exploratory discussion. Avni recalled: "I then went into one of my frenzies, where I figured it I don't get this, the world is going to collapse."[29] After frantic pleas from Avni and letters from Equity, Avni was given permission by the Odets estate.

The play's next problem was that Polan had cast a working actress named Teresa Hughes, a temperamental, arrogant, inconsistent actress, according to Avni, who made Polan's life miserable. Finally, Avni agreed with Polan that it was best to replace the actress. A week before the play opened, they hired Vera Lockwood, who had performed the drama earlier at the Roundabout Theater. The difficulty was that Lockwood initially read the part in a Yiddish accent. Avni spoke to her quietly, explaining that the family in *Awake and Sing!* would not have had Yiddish accents, and that the JRT had been founded, specifically, to foster the idea that Jews should not be portrayed as stereotypes. All Jews, in fact, do not have Yiddish accents.

The play also brought back such regulars as set designer Jeffrey Schneider and costume designer Karen Hummel and actor Michael Albert Mantel, who recalled it as his best experience at the JRT and as a pivotal point in the theater's career. "When I first read the play, I thought, 'This play is about me.' It gave me a sense of belonging, of tradition."[30] Polan also recalled it as a highlight:

> It was a wonderful production, with the combination of
> the level of acting and the material itself. I loved working on it, and a lot of famous people came to see it.[31]

As Avni pointed out, the *New York Times* gave the JRT the best review it had ever had, praising the show far above the earlier Roundabout production:

> If there is any show that is difficult to make electric in
> revival, it is "Awake and Sing!", that Clifford Odets
> drama-poem of the Bronx that established so many
> cliches of dialogue for succeeding playwrights that it
> might seem to parody itself. For all that, the Jewish
> Repertory Theatre, which frequently sets currents pulsing in its modest East 14th Street house, has done it again
> with a production of this fine old chestnut that makes one
> awake and sing.[32]

While the Jewish press was more critical of the play itself, finding
the play dated and the situations pallid, it did give high grades to the
performances.[33]

In December, a new play, *Elephants*, which had grown out of Edward Cohen's Writers' Lab, was directed by Cohen. Chicago writer
David Rush had sent Cohen the script the previous year, and the two
had worked on revisions over the phone.

The three-character drama deals with the aging janitor of a Chicago
synagogue, his estranged son, and a bag lady. The janitor steals cocaine to finance a trip to Israel to see his dying sister, and enlists the
bag lady's help. Both are embittered, lonely characters who have lost
their families through their own stubbornness. Loneliness that people
bring upon themselves through indifference to others is the play's
theme.

Cohen recruited two veteran actors, the competent husband-wife
team of Lee Wallace and Marilyn Chris, and Richard Niles for the
son's role. Avni recalled that the audiences enjoyed the play, but critics responded to the production with mixed reviews—positive comments on the acting and negative comments on the play itself. The
New York Times found the animal symbols pretentious and added:

> The play would be dismissable were it not for the
> presence on stage of Lee Wallace and Marilyn
> Chris.... With little help from the playwright, but an as-
> sist from their director, Edward M. Cohen, the two create
> a double portrait of self-imposed loneli-
> ness.... Unfortunately, the mutually responsice perfor-
> mances cannot transcend the manipulative script.
> Watching Mr. Wallace and Miss Chris in *Elephants*, one
> wishes that they were in a play equal to their artistry.[34]

A Long Island paper had a kinder response:

> ...with deft touches of humor interwoven into the fabric
> of this cheerless situation, Rush's play asks painful ques-
> tions and offers moral options it might be well for all of
> us to contemplate.[35]

Debbi Wasserman added that the play was a serious study of loneliness and old age, but that it was "a bit self-consciously commercial,
with an inclination towards compact, neat explanations, but in the
hands of the Jewish Repertory Theatre, these transgressions are easily

overlooked.''[36]

In January 1982 a children's theater, loosely connected with the JRT, at least in name, was launched. It was called the Jewish Rep for Young Audiences and was directed by Joyce Klein, who took her productions around to the New York City schools. Her programs consisted of skits and plays focusing on Jewish themes.

February saw a "world premier" of two plays involving the poet Delmore Schwartz. One was a short play by Schwartz himself entitled *Shenandoah*, and the other, *Luna Park*, was a play, based on a Schwartz story *In Dreams Begin Responsibilities*, and written by the young playwright Donald Margulies. Both were directed by actress Florence Stanley. Two years earlier Stanley had brought the Schwartz play to the JRT with the hope of directing it. She and Avni decided that the short play would have to be paired with another, and Cohen, recalling Margulies's work, suggested that he write a companion piece based on a Schwartz story. The result was Margulies's *Luna Park*, which was given a staged reading that season. (For a more detailed discussion of this production, see Chapter 5.)

Luna Park, the curtain-raiser, is a memory piece that concerns the poet's vision of his parent's courtship, and *Shenandoah*, the longer Schwartz play, is a comedy about Jews striving to become Americanized and focusses on the naming of an infant at a circumcision ritual.

Avni recalled that the production came close to closing before it ever opened, because of his differences with Florence Stanley:

> That was the year that a number of theaters gave first-time chances to actresses to direct. So I said, "If it's good for the Manhattan Theater Club, it can be good for us." But it was a horrendous experience, because of the tech time. She was bringing on a whole new set of furniture for each scene, a beginner-type of approach for set changes, but one that was soluble by slightly altering the concept. This was the first and only time where I gave the director an ultimatum, saying that we can't have those black-outs. She said, "Are you saying that if I don't cut the black-outs, we're not going to open?" I said, "Yes!" Of course in the end she agreed....But we've remained kind of friends. She's still on our board and comes to shows.[37]

Nevertheless, the critics had high praise for Stanley. One comments:

> Veteran actress Florence Stanley, here directing for the first time, has infused her whole cast with her own acute, flexible sense of comic timing and the results are beautiful. [38]

Elenore Lester added that the Margulies adaptation served as an important prologue to the Schwartz play, the stronger of the two, which offered sensitive insight into family life, and that "both plays moved well under the direction of Florence Stanley." [39] Avni himself summarized the production and its two plays by saying that *Shenandoah* was "terrific and well done." As to *Luna Park*, "I wasn't crazy about it, but people kind of liked it." [40]

The spring production was an avant-garde play *Pantagleize* by Belgian playwright Michel De Ghelderode, directed by Anthony McKay. The 1929 play was a dark farce about leftist revolution. Pantagleize, a fashion writer, is mistaken for a revolutionary leader and inadvertently gives the secret phrase that launches his country's revolution.

"It was an allegory, an off-the-wall, wacky play you couldn't make realistic sense of," said Avni. "A Jewess is a leading character, and we took it as a metaphor. The Jews are used to instigate revolution and social change, and, when there's no further use for them, they are disposed of." [41]

Critic Howard Waxman praised McKay's work and found the play intriguing:

> Director Anthony McKay has staged this European classic with the theatrical flair it deserves, realizing the sense of the absurd that marks De Ghelderode's contribution to the theater of the twentieth century. [42]

But Avni saw it as a "respectable failure."

> I loved the production itself. I was very proud of it. But the play was outdated. This was one of the first Brechtian type of plays, where you depicted the revolution and said how bad Fascism was. But we've seen too many plays like that, and it just wasn't good enough drama. [43]

The JRT's June production proved to be a major hit, extending its run through the summer, with a mini-contract for the extended run and with actors receiving a weekly salary of $124.72. With almost 8000 people seeing the show, and expenses relatively low, it earned a dazzling $70,500 in box office receipts. (The theater's largest receipts until that time were $19,600 for *36*, a comedy about the last saint, presented in the 1979-1980 season.)

The show was *Vagabond Stars*, directed by Avni and combining the efforts of writer Nahma Sandrow, composer/arranger Raphael Crystal, lyricist Alan Poul, choreographer Bick Goss, set designer Jeffrey Schneider, lighting designer Phil Monat, and costume designer Karen Hummel. Both Avni and Cohen were deeply involved in developing the script. The cast of five performers, playing many roles, included Susan Victor, who later performed in many other JRT productions.

The show was an English-language adaptation of Yiddish songs, sketches, and dramatic scenes—a musical revue tied together by the theme of the Jewish immigrant experience. The name came from Nahma Sandrow's 1977 book on the history of Yiddish theater. Sandrow later wrote a show of the same name, translating stories and songs from the Yiddish theater. The show, which had had a modest success in the Berkshires, became a new production at the JRT, retaining the name but greatly changed:

> I met Nahma, and we talked about new concepts. She came up with the idea that it takes place in an old Yiddish theater. Finally, I said, "My God, let's take only the material that deals directly with the immigration, putting it in order, starting with people on the boat. The correct order will tell the story."[44]

Although composer Raphael Crystal had worked on the original *Vagabond Stars* in the Berkshires, the JRT version became his first contact with Avni's theater. The association would continue with other musicals, proving to be fruitful for all concerned. A versatile, brilliant composer, Crystal had graduated from Harvard University with a music degree and went on to study musical theater at Queens College. His work in the field has included teaching, writing, and especially musical directing for theatrical productions. As a composer he was launched at Ellen Stewart's La Mama, when she presented his oratorio *Noah*.

Vagabond Stars had a special significance for Crystal in terms of his own heritage. Both his father and his uncle had been involved with Yiddish theater as publicists and translators, and both later became journalists for the Yiddish press. For many years, his father, Morris Crystal, was editor-in-chief of the *Jewish Daily Forward*.

Crystal's contribution to *Vagabond Stars* became more than a re-working of old songs:

> We put things together to make new numbers. it was a process of going through old material and reinventing it. The problems were chiefly with the lyrics. How do you do a translation that keeps the flavor, but also is a good translation and functions well in English? You want something clever and erudite that works in English, but recalls the original.[45]

Vagabond Stars proved to be a huge success with critics. The *New York Times* reviewer wrote: "It's impossible not to be charmed by *Vagabond Stars*, the Jewish Repertory Theatre's bright new musical, so why even try?"[46] The *New York Daily News* saw it as "a charming memory lane of skits, blackouts, sentimental tunes and memories of old New York."[47] And the *New York Post* found it "a warm and charming entertainment, full of nostalgic affection for the people who created it out of their own lives."[48] "*Vagabond Stars* was an exciting night at the theater," another critic wrote. "It's too bad the rest of the world (seemingly) won't give equal time to old fashioned theater events such as *Vagabond*; it's the rest of the world that misses out."[49] And the *Jewish Press* added: "These days, it's not often that a play comes along that's Jewish, delightful, moving and memorable; so *Vagabond Stars* is an unexpected delight."[50]

While there was some talk of an uptown commercial production, nothing came of it. As Avni saw it, the production did not have enough commercial potential, despite the charming Yiddish songs, to bring in non-Jewish audiences and fill a large theater at expensive uptown prices.

But *Vagabond Stars* succeeded on its home territory, and, with its success, the JRT moved into high finance. At that point Don Geller began to keep a serious itemized acount of expenses and income for the theater. He listed actual figures where he could, but had to estimate amounts for YMHA services to the theater. For example, it was very difficult for Geller to calculate how many hours of clerical and maintenance work the Y office provided for the JRT. Nevertheless, Geller determined that for the 1981-1982 season the JRT had incurred $116,319 in expenses. That included $66,840 for personnel, about $11,000 for marketing and about $18,000 for production expenses. Against expenses, the JRT had brought in $61,734 (*Vagabond Stars* summer receipts were included in the following year), and a $54,585 earning gap had to be made up by Y contributions in services, grants and Y board and individual contributions. Like all non-profit theaters, the JRT was operating at a deficit, despite its healthy box office returns. The greater its success, the larger the deficits, Geller said complainingly.[51]

That summer, while *Vagabond Stars* continued to play at home, the JRT took part in the first International Conference and Festival of Jewish Theatre in Israel. They presented a staged reading of Grace Paley's *The Loves of Shirley Abramowitz*, with actress Susan Merson, directed by Edward Cohen. (Cohen had worked with Paley on the script in his Writers' Lab and had given it a staged reading.) The Festival featured seminars and performance groups from England, Europe, the United States and Israel. Avni attended because, he said, his fare and accommodations were paid and he stayed for the first time in his life at the Hilton Hotel in Israel, a luxury for him. But he had little use for the Festival and felt that the sponsor, the National Foundation for Jewish Culture, should have spent the money differently, by giving it directly to theaters.[52]

1982-1983

The 1982-83 season saw several changes: audience subscriptions, which had remained fairly constant the previous year had jumped, with the boost from *Vagabond Stars*, from last season's figure of about 680 to over 800. And Edward Cohen's work with playwrights also moved forward. That season he would work with and help develop the scripts of some sixteen writers and several composers. Both Raphael Crystal and Margaret Pine (who had worked with Cohen on earlier productions and works-in-progress) would become composers-in-residence, with a more regular commitment to the JRT. And Cohen, with the help of a grant, would officially launch his Playwrights-in-Residence program. (See Chapter 5 of this study.) The theater itself continued on its Tier Two Equity contract, paying actors $230 per show.

As to productions, the JRT opened with Arthur Miller's *After the Fall* directed by William Shroder. At the insistence of Denise Lute, a frequent JRT actress, Avni met Shroder, a successful Florida builder who directed community theater in Sarasota. Lute kept insisting that Shroder was a fine man and, despite a lack of professional experience, a good director. They finally made contact, and Shroder, who had dreams of directing a New York show, offered to fly Avni down to Florida to see the production of *After the Fall* that he was directing there. On seeing the show Avni thought it was indeed a possibility for the JRT.[53]

Shroder had tightened and adapted the script and directed the show in a way that Avni liked. At Avni's suggestion Shroder sent the script to Miller, who like the changes enough to agree to meet with both in New York City. "He took Miller and me to dinner at the Cote Basque. Bill and I were in proper suits and ties, and there was Miller in an old turtle neck and corduroy jacket. The upshot was that Miller agreed to let Bill direct the play."[54]

Because Shroder was a well-to-do man and wanted the best possible production, he contributed money to the effort so that they could hire a press agent, have a more elaborate set and go to mini-contract, with actors paid on a weekly basis (including rehearsals).

The play itself, clearly autoboigraphical, relates the stormy marriage of a playwright and his celebrity/actress wife (Miller and second wife Marilyn Monroe). Critics have said that Miller was too close to the material, the end result being a play that was unstructured, long-winded, and obtuse.

Nonetheless, Shroder had a good production, in Avni's view, with several JRT regulars on hand to help it succeed—set designer Jeffrey Schneider and costume designer Karen Hummel, as well as Avni himself.

> His only difficulty was in casting the lead. He couldn't get out of his mind that woman who had played the lead in Sarasota, so he brought her up from Florida. But the problem was he had not seen her in over a year, she had gained 20 pounds, and she looked like a hick. He put her on the stage with sharp, accomplished New York actors, and right away there were problems.[55]

Shroder eventually fired the actress, replacing her with the actress he had liked in auditions, Kathy Rosseter. Miller liked the production, although not as well as *Incident at Vichy*. He complained, said Avni, "that Martin Shakar, who played the lead, was too internal, with a lot happening inside but not enough outside. That was what Marilyn Monroe considered the ultimate acting, but I guess not Miller."[56]

Shroder's big disappointment was that the *New York Times* did not review the show, although it received favorable reviews, on the whole, from the Jewish press and other smaller New York papers, with the *Village Voice* commenting that the play was sexist and "embarrassingly self-serving" but the production good.[57]

Nonetheless, Shroder returned to Florida, feeling that it had been the best interval of his life. Avni had given him a priceless experience.[58]

The December show featured another Edward Cohen project. A year earlier two young playwrights (also named Cohen—Neil and Joel) had brought a comedy entitled *Friends Too Numerous to Mention* to Cohen. It dealt with a theater-owner's attempts to maintain a theater in the suburbs with support from the crime syndicate.

It was a long play with many characters, but it got the Cohen treatment, with a staged reading and his suggestions to cut this and do that. They reworked it, brought it back, with Allen Coulter, a friend of theirs, to direct.[59]

Avni, pleased to have another controversial play on stage, gave it his blessing.

Reviewer Richard Shepard liked the play:

What could be tragedy...has been made into high comedy with sharp insights into human behavior abetted by good, snappy lines, a fast-moving production and a cast that throws itself joyously into the action.[60]

The *New York Post* saw the play as "a situation ripe with comic possibilities," one that would make "a nifty TV pilot," although it was not full enough for its stage length.[61]

Based on the favorable *New York Times* review, the playwrights wanted to extend the play, but Avni refused, pointing out that, despite the review, attendance did not warrant an extension, which would have meant going to mini-contract. It would be a losing proposition.

Joel Cohen was furious with the hard-headed practical decision.

The first production in 1983 was a revival of Anton Chekhov's *Ivanov*. Originally Avni had hoped to put Clifford Odets's play *Paradise Lost* into the February slot, and had in fact negotiated with the agency handling the Odets estate, but ultimately found that he could not get permission. Once again, Avni felt they were on the verge of disaster. They had already lined up Anthony McKay as a director and they needed a February show. Avni and Cohen considered bringing back one of their earlier successes—possibly Chayevsky's *Middle of the Night* (produced in September 1976) or *Ivanov* (produced in June 1977). Finding they could not get the rights to the Chayevsky play, they asked McKay about directing *Ivanov* and found he was eager for the opportunity. "It was a time when we could still afford a big cast, so the play was feasible," said Avni.[62]

McKay assembled a highly competent cast of eighteen, most of whom were new to the JRT but seasoned Equity professionals, including Michael Mantel, who at that point was also an Equity actor.

McKay found it a positive experience and, again, enjoyed the openly-expressed audience reaction:

> When Ivanov, infuriated with his wife, says, "You Jewess!" one woman in the audience turned to her husband and said, "See!" She had been waiting for Ivanov all along to turn on his wife.[63]

Although not covered by major papers (except for advance billing), the smaller New York papers reviewed the show favorably. One critic praised the production for its brisk direction and fine performances,[64] and another critic pointed out that the JRT had given audiences a rare opportunity to see a seldom-performed Chekhov play, adding that the "JRT has turned a minor Chekhov play into a fine evening of theater."[65]

The April show was an Edward Cohen production from start to finish, under his directon and co-written by two of his protege playwrights—Canadian Kenneth Klonsky and Brian Shein. Both were among the many playwrights Cohen helped along the way, although they did not become JRT playwrights-in-residence.

Entitled *Taking Steam*, the comedy takes place in a dilapidated YMHA health club in Toronto. The play is similar in environment— but environment only—to the British import *Steaming*, which reached

Broadway at about the same time. The play focusses not on nubile, nude young women but rather, on towel-wrapped older Jewish men. And the play deals with such issues as fidelity, aging, retirement.

Taking Steam was particularly notable for its realistic set, designed by Adalberto Ortiz, so authentic, in fact, that some viewers thought the play had actually been moved to the locker room at the Y.

Avni recalled the comedy as "a mild success," appealing to some, but not all viewers. While some liked the authenticity, others disliked the occasional profanity and still others questioned, "Why do I have to go to the theater to see a health club?"[66]

As to the critics' reactions, Richard Shepard found its realistic set, direction, and acting appealing:

> It is a good slice of life, a two-act vignette, perhaps, rather
> than a full-blown play, and one that unerringly rings true,
> down to its very feel, intonations and inflections.[67]

In all, it did not go on to a commercial life, as the directors and writers had hoped, but Cohen did direct a production of the play later that year in Toronto.

Meanwhile Raphael Crystal was already at work on another musical. It had, by this time, become a JRT tradition to complete each season with a musical. (There was always the possibility that if it was successful, it could be extended into the summer.) It was Crystal's idea to do a work focussing, not on Ashkanazim Jews, but on the Sephardim, using authentic Spanish music.[68]

Avni was dubious until Crystal suggested using the story of Judah Halevy, a 12th-century poet and physician. Avni was intrigued and planned to direct the show. The story would be Jewish, but a more unusual, exotic kind of Jewishness. American Jews knew little about the Sephardim, he felt, and the idea had good possibilities.

Crystal proceeded, after several unsuccessful attempts, to find a book writer, Linda Kline, and a lyricist, Richard Engquist. Avni was not happy with Kline's work, but in the face of imminent deadlines, he felt he had little choice:

> She didn't have the real feeling for the lead character or
> what he was about. She kept focussing on his girl friend
> back in Spain, when the whole point of the story was that
> this guy spent his life yearning for Zion because he
> couldn't take the hypocrisy of living successfully in

Spain—a lot like America today.[69]

The musical was called *My Heart Is in the East*. The first act was concerned with Halevy's life in Cordoba, Spain, and the second half with his overseas travels—with dalliance in Egypt and finally embarkation for Jerusalem.

According to Avni, the story was artificial, but the music and lyrics were glorious, a view with which critic Richard Shepard concurred, referring to it as a "musical that suffers from that most perennial of musical ailments, a weak book. It is better sung than spoken."[70]

It was, in fact, the beginning of the highly successful Crystal/ Engquist team. Other JRT regulars on hand were set designer Jeffrey Schneider, costume designer Karen Hummel and performer Susan Victor. Another find for the JRT was Haila Strauss, who came in midway through rehearsals, replacing an unsatisfactory choreographer.

The *New York Post* also praised the production, with its clever set, romantic lighting, and small, versatile cast, and said in summation that "Ran Avni's production is the essence of vitality."[71]

In all, despite its shortcomings, audiences liked the show, and, on the strength of their reactions and the good *New York Post* review, the JRT decided to extend the musical into the summer.

It was a mistake. *My Heart Is in the East* ran for 12 more performances in July, bringing in only 443 people and a gate of some $4700, very small indeed compared to earlier summer runs. *Vagabond Stars*, for example, had earned $55,708 in its summer run, and even *36* almost $15,000 in its extension. Moreover, expenses were higher, with Equity having increased actors' salaries in January 1983 to $132.08 weekly for special extended runs under a mini-contract. "We lost our shirt," said Avni, "because the review appeared on the Fourth of July week-end and no one was in town to read it."[72]

But overall, the 1982-1983 season showed a box office return that had doubled that of the previous year, with a total of $122,000. However, expenses had mounted as well, and Don Geller continued to complain that the more successful the JRT was, the more expensive it was for the Y. Productions had become more elaborate, with the help of more professional theater people. The total expenses for the season were over $211,000, with almost half of that money going for artistic and technical personnel. But, with Y support, the JRT

met its budget. The Y had contributed in-kind services estimated at
$35,800, and its board members had joined others to bring in a to-
tal of $31,000 in contributions. It was also the year that Edward Cohen
received a $10,000 National Endowment for the Arts grant to set up
his playwrights' program (see Chapter 5) and the New York Coun-
cil on the Arts awarded the theater $11,000.

1983-1984

Beginning with the 1983-1984 season, the JRT moved to a mini-
contract for all its shows, not just for its extended runs. Actors, directors, and technical people were paid on a weekly basis, rehearsals
included. At the beginning of the year Actors' Equity Association
had imposed a cost of living increase on salaries, bringing the actors' salaries for the JRT up to $117.08 weekly for regular mini-
contract runs, with technical people slightly higher. The theater was
also responsible for pension fund and welfare fund payments.
Although the amounts were small from a working actor's point of
view, they represented a considerable increase in expenses for the
theater.

The season opened with Arthur Miller's *Up From Paradise*, a musical based on his Book of Genesis play, *The Creation of the World
and Other Business*. The book and lyrics were written by Miller himself and the music by Stanley Silverman. The musical had been performed in concert at the Whitney Museum, but never before on stage
in New York. Featuring Broadway actors and with music played by
the Verona Wind Quartet, it was, as Alfred Plant wrote in a letter
to subscribers, "the most ambitious production that we have ever
presented."[73]

When Avni had called Miller's agent Bridget Aschenberg of International Creative Management, Inc. the previous spring seeking
another Miller play, she suggested the musical. Miller was happy
to have Avni direct, but Silverman, who had never seen Avni's work,
had reservations. He and Aschenberg went to see *My Heart Is in the
East*, which they hated, according to Avni. They interviewed other
directors, but found no one they liked. Avni finally convinced them
that "you are not going to find a better director than me."[74]

Silverman finally agreed, but insisted that he himself do the choreography. Avni was not totally happy with the arrangement, but de-

cided privately that he would keep the choreography to a minimum.

Avni went to Israel that summer on his honeymoon, following his marriage to Lori Schainuck. He had met his future wife three years earlier when she had just graduated from Sarah Lawrence College. Again, as in so many other fortuitous JRT meetings, Gerry Lou Silverman was to be the catalyst, bringing the two together. It would prove to be a strong, supportive marriage with Lori's patience and understanding helping Ran Avni through many difficult times at the JRT. He took the script and tapes with him. He returned, filled with excitement and ideas for the production.

As casting got under way, Silverman told Avni that Austin Pendleton was upset he had not been offered the Adam role, which he had read at the Museum. Avni doubted that Pendleton would be willing to perform at the JRT, but when he approached the actor, he agreed at once. Armed with Pendleton, he then asked Len Cariou (who had earlier won the Tony award for *Sweeney Todd*) to play God. Cariou also agreed, as did Alice Playten, who had also performed in the Whitney concert. Needing a young man for Abel, he went to Lonny Price and "before I knew it, I was sitting on a pot of gold. It turned out to be a magnificent production, an exciting evening of theater, in many respects."[75]

Avni admitted that the play itself—basically the retelling of the story of creation without a "new angle"—was problematic. But he felt that the production was an achievement in terms of adapting and tailoring a large-size story and musical to a small stage. His directing, he felt, was "brilliant":

> Most critics mentioned how great the direction was—except Frank Rich, who paid his first visit to the theater. He attacked it savagely, saying it looked like a Bar Mitzvoh with a shortage of chairs. Actually, whatever "Up From Paradise" was, there was nothing in it that resembled any Jewish rituals.[76]

Nevertheless, the very fact that Rich attended at all gave added prestige to the JRT. And whether or not the Rich review was a personal attack is of course open to question. But the review was indeed negative on all counts, with the show summarized as "a casual, warm-spirited and innocuous musical chalk talk whose future is likely to reside with amateur church and synagogue groups."[77]

The musical was widely covered in the New York area and in national papers, as well as the *New Yorker* and *New York Magazine*, undoubtedly because of the prestige of the playwright and cast. The critics in general gave limited praise to the production, but less to the play. Only John Simon, who clearly had little regard for the playwright, was as devastating as Rich, commenting that "there is no more wit or desirability or point to the revision than to the original."[78] But Edith Oliver praised the rich melodic score, the performances, the direction,[79] and John Beaufort summarized, "Although Mr. Miller's jocular liberties may prove too flippant for some and his perceptions not profound enough for others, *Up From Paradise* deserves the care and skill Mr. Avni and his colleagues have lavished on it."[80] And Linda Winer wrote: "It is no big deal, but Miller's first and only musical is a seriously endearing little cabaret and cantata—hip, relaxed and cast with a childlike affirmation of heaven."[81]

Despite the mixed critical reactions, Avni felt he had moved into the "big league" with the Miller musical. Moreover, audience attendance was strong, and total gate receipts at $22,317 topped any other previous show (with the exception of *Vagabond Stars*).

The JRT went on to a December production of *Gifted Children* by the promising young playwright Donald Margulies, whose earlier work on Delmore Schwartz had been staged at the JRT and who continued to work with Cohen. The production was directed by Joan Vail Thorne and featured award-winning players of stage, film, and television, Dinah Manoff and Zohra Lampert. Ben Siegler, the third actor, was also a seasoned actor. Yet, despite such credentials, the production evoked a tepid reaction from critics and audiences. "Audiences didn't love it, but they didn't hate it," said Avni. "They didn't walk out."[82]

The play dealt with a love-hate mother-daughter relationship, and the need for the daughter to separate herself from this intense relationship in order to find her own identity. The *New York Times* review praised Manoff's performance, but saw the play itself as amateurish and Lampert's performance as dreadful:

> Even this actress's mannerisms have mannerisms: She
> adds at least four syllables to every monosyllabic word,
> waves her hands incessantly and whines in a guttural

growl that sounds like a flooding car carburetor.[83]

Margulies was unhappy with Lampert's performance, as was Avni, who said, "Whether or not the show worked depended on Zohra, and she was kind of a *meshugenah*. When she was 'on,' she was spectacular, but when she was 'off,' she was horrible, and Rich saw her on an off night."[84]

But critic Don Nelsen was kinder to the play, seeing it as a step beyond the usual parent-child alienation:

> Margulies examines the consequences of failed dreams as they are passed unwittingly from one generation to the next almost as a matter of tradition.... Margulies draws his characters in more than one dimension but he is done in by one poor performance: in the part of a desperate mother, Zohra Lampert gives us little more than a caricatured Jewish mother stereotype.[85]

The smaller neighborhood papers, on the other hand, found the play itself gifted and even enjoyed Lampert's performance.

Once again, in the next production, the JRT moved into Pinter's world. Harold Pinter's *The Homecoming*, directed by Anthony McKay, was the February 1984 choice, and, Avni, using one of his favorite adjectives, called it a "brilliant production."[86]

Although audiences and critics had had reservations about the JRT's earlier Pinter production, *The Birthday Party*, directed by Anthony McKay in February 1981, Avni himself recalled the production in positive terms. And he felt more strongly than ever that Pinter was appropriate territory for the JRT to explore:

> This is the very essence of the JRT idea. This whole theater, to begin with, was to find new, untraditional, unconventional ways of dealing with Jewishness— illuminating and exploring and redefining the Jewish experience. That, in some ways, is what Pinter tried to do for himself—to redefine what it meant to be Jewish, or to deal with the Jewish aspect of his personality.[87]

Jewish themes are in fact even more apparent in *The Homecoming* than in *The Birthday Party*. Although there are no openly Jewish characters, as with Golberg in *The Birthday Party*, the implications clearly exist. Pinter gives all his characters Jewish-type names such as Sam and Lennie, and he makes the father Max a butcher, certainly a likely occupation for certain classes of London Jews. Most importantly, Pinter's story of a woman returning to the land of her husband, choosing to live among her husband's people, is the Biblical story of Ruth. Pinter has turned the story inside out, giving it a shock treatment, but it is Old Testament, a Jewish story, all the same.

Furthermore, a case could be made for *The Homecoming* being a metaphor for the founding of the state of Israel. In returning to their homeland, as they see it, Jews have had to deal with a special kind of "homecoming," a hostile reception from the Arabs, and have lived in a perpetual state of war not unlike Pinter's "homecoming."

The play, vintage Pinter, deals with a philosophy professor and his wife who returns unexpectedly from America to his bizarre family and their London home. The wife decides to stay on as live-in whore for the father and two brothers—one a small-time pimp and the other a would-be boxer. Such is Pinter's menacing, absurdist world and puzzling plot.

There were other reasons for Avni's choice of a Pinter play. In planning the season, he and Cohen looked for established plays with small casts, since a full season of new plays was a dangerous box office risk. Moreover, Avni admired the directorial skills of McKay, who was pleased to do another Pinter play.

While Avni admired the production whole-heartedly, the predominant audience reaction was one of respect, mixed with bewilderment.

Critics' reactions were entirely positive. Enthusiasm for the veteran award-winning actor Joe Silver, in the lead role of Max, was particularly strong:

> Harold Pinter never makes it easy for an audience to accept and swallow his plots. But the acting, most particularly that of Joe Silver, finds you first questioning, yet ultimately accepting them. It would be difficult to find someone today with so wonderfully trained a voice and with such tremendous skill as a character actor as Joe Silver.[88]

And the *New York Times* considered it a fine revival, where everything, including the enigmatic pauses, still worked. "It almost comes as a bonus that the acting and the direction, by Anthony McKay, are

uniformly professional and faithful to the play's fundamental ir-
rationality.''[89]

The spring 1984 production, *Escape from Riverdale*, came out of
Edward Cohen's playwright's group (see Chapter 5) as did the earlier
show *Gifted Children*. Cohen had assisted and advised playwright
Don Wollner, another promising young playwright, with the script.
Returning to the JRT was Lynn Polan as director and Michael Al-
bert Mantel in a lead role.

Billed as a single play, it was actually two one-act dramas, united
by the same lead character in both plays and by the common theme
of growing up and getting out of Riverdale. All the characters are
rich Jewish suburban adolescents.

While critic Richard Shepard praised the direction and performances, he deplored the play itself:

> There may be a play with an idea rattling around...but
> it hasn't made a good enough connection on its flight from
> uptown to downtown....It has some impressive perfor-
> mances and moments, too few, when the dialogue catches
> the ear nicely. There are even points of tension in its evo-
> cation of a restless time for American youth. But it fails
> in its attempts to imitate J.D. Salinger and Woody
> Allen.[90]

In all, it was not successful with audiences either, for they disliked
the subject matter and did not like to see Jewish adolescents portrayed
in that manner. (See Chapter 6 for a discussion of audience reaction
to *Escape from Riverdale*.)

But the season ended with a bang. *Kuni-Leml*, the theater's June
production, directed by Avni, became its all-time hit, both financially and critically, and may well be the JRT's best-remembered
show in years to come. It went on to an extended summer run, with
box office receipts of over $100,000, followed by an uptown the-
ater district production, staging in other parts of the United States
and Canada, as well as plans for a production in Israel.

The idea took shape following the success of *Vagabond Stars* and
took almost two years to come to fruition. Avni suggested to Raphael
Crystal that he look at one of the well-known Yiddish writers and
composers and perhaps do a musical. The first name that came to
mind for both was Avrom Goldfadn, the man considered to be the

father of Yiddish theater. Crystal worked for some time assembling Goldfadn songs and met with Avni one evening to play the material. "They all sounded the same, with seven chords, it seemed, used for all the songs," said Avni. "I thought that it would make an awfully boring evening!"[91]

They decided, instead, to take an actual Goldfadn play, to be translated and adapted into a musical, with original music added. They considered one called *The Witch* but finally agreed upon *The Two Kumi-Lemls*. Avni was aware of the long-lasting popularity of the play.

The story is set in nineteenth-century Odessa and concerns a free-thinking young woman who rebels against tradition. Her rabbi father has chosen for her husband one Kuni-Leml. The father sees him as the perfect choice, because he is a pious Jew from a distinguished religious family. In reality, he is the ultimate simpleton[92] with an outrageous list of physical deformities. She of course prefers a handsome young student as her suitor. The play, following a tradition that dates back to early Roman theater, is a fast-moving farce of deception and mistaken identities.

As a next step Avni and Crystal approached the writers of *Vagabond Stars*, Nahma Sandrow and Alan Poul. Sandrow agreed to do the translation and book if the JRT would apply for a translator grant under the NEA, which she would then share with the other two. They applied for a $12,000 grant but received only $6000. Split three ways, it meant only $2000 for each, so the JRT agreed to match the grant, so that each writer received a total of $4000.

> We commissioned it. Unfortunately, we didn't put anything in contract form, which would have helped us at a later point, in terms of owning the property. But that's how you learn.[93]

It was that winter, as the trio was about to get under way, that Crystal called Avni in Florida to say that Alan Poul had had another offer. Would Avni mind if he called in Richard Engquist as a replacement? Avni, who knew Engquist's work from *My Heart Is in the East*, agreed, and work on the show began.

Sandrow initially wrote a synopsis of the original play, condensing it with Cohen's help and, working with the composer and lyricist, they determined where the songs could carry the story. Avni, upon hearing the new songs, thought they were wonderful. But they were yet to realize that the fledgling show had enormous commercial potential. Nor did any of them realize, until Sandrow pointed it out, that this was the first major Yiddish work for the stage to be translated into English.

As casting got under way, Avni began to realize that he had something special. Performers were eager to get into the show. Avni did not think that Broadway actor Gene Varrone, for example, would take the relatively minor role of the matchmaker, but he did. Other seasoned performers in the cast included Mark Zeller, Barbara McCulloh, Scott Wentworth, Susan Victor, and Stuart Zagnit as Kuni-Leml. Once gain Karen Hummel did the costumes and Haila Strauss the musical staging.

As rehearsal went forward, scenes had to be smoothed out and changed. Avni decided to change the chorus of three students into a pair:

> It reinforced the concept that everything was in pairs, that
> everybody imitated everybody else. I had to fight with
> the writers about it, but after the first rehearsal, I felt we
> had a very big hit.[94]

There were contract problems from the beginning, partly because Avni did not have an attorney. Finally, they took an old contract left over from an earlier show, following the format, and Avni signed with the writers. The arrangement was that the production would run as long as possible at the JRT, without extra royalties to the writers, since they had received the original commission money.

The show opened on June 9 to rave reviews, as Avni had anticipated. Richard Shepard's review set the tone, for the many other reviewers, when he said that "the production sings," and that it was a "warm, high-spirited evening of comedy." He added that the show was an "expertly crafted tuneful presentation that, blending two old traditions, the Yiddish and the operetta, is a thoroughly modern effort."[95] The *Village Voice* echoed those sentiments:

> The production is impeccable. Raphael Crystal has in-
> corporated some of Goldfadn's tunes and lyrics into his
> score, which, like everything else in the piece, is both
> a homage to and conversation with the past.[96]

And Leora Mann's review added whatever else had to be said:

The current production, under Ran Avni's sharp direction, conveys the message with a charming cast of characters, lilting musical numbers, and most of all, a wonderful
sense of humor.[97]

On the basis of such reviews and audience reaction, the JRT extended the run, and the show ran, in fact, throughout the summer
for a total of 87 performances.

Almost from the beginning, Avni said, producers began to come
in to see the show, to consider its uptown possibilties, and many were
interested. The one who was ready to talk seriously, both as a theater owner and co-producer, was Jack Lawrence, owner of the
Audrey Wood Theater on West 48th Street. Avni met with Lawrence
at a restaurant to pursue the possibility of a jointly-sponsored production. They began negotiations, but Avni had already made plans to
go to Israel for a summer vacation, and Alfred Plant took over the
negotiations.

The final agreement was to move the show, intact, uptown to
Lawrence's theater in the fall. The show was capitalized at $125,000,
with Lawrence raising $50,000 and Plant, as chairman of the JRT
board, raising $75,000.

It was a bad deal for us percentagewise because we raised
two-thirds of the money but only had fifty percent of the
profits, which didn't turn out to be much anyway. Besides we gave Jack all the financial decisions, and we retained all the artistic decisions. There were lots of fights
and haggling, but when I came back from Israel, my cab
from the airport stopped at the toll booth where I got a
paper. I read the item in the *Times* Broadway column that
the show was opening on October 9. That was heart-
warming.[98]

The uptown show, with the same cast, opened at the 200-seat theater on October 9, with reviews as enthusiastic as they had been for
the 14th Street Y production. Mel Gussow referred to the musical
as "a kind of vest-pocket equivalent of *Fiddler on the Roof*" and "a
compact musical, as unpretentious as it is ingratiating."[99] Marilyn
Stasio said, "We're talking very old-fashioned, here—but really well
done."[100] And *Variety* added, "You don't have to be Jewish to enjoy *Kuni-Leml*, a delightful and captivating fast-paced musical."[101]

The show enjoyed a solid run, closing on April 21, 1985. Ran Avni and the theater went on to win a number of awards for *Kuni-Leml*. It took that year's Outer Critics Circle Award for best lyrics, best music and best musical off-Broadway. And it was cited in *The Burns Mantle Yearbook, The Best Plays of 1984-85* for best musical (together with *Big River*), best lyricist (Richard Engquist), best book (Nahma Sandrow), and best director (Ran Avni) for both Broadway and off-Broadway.[102]

Kuni-Leml has since played in many places and with many productions, continuing to provide royalties for its writers, with twenty percent of those royalties for the JRT. But the JRT has benefited in other ways, in terms of the highly profitable summer run, the greater prestige and recognition, and a doubling of the subscriber list.

While 1983-1984 was significant to the JRT because of its biggest hit, it did not come out so well for the year's earnings and expenses. An explanation is that *My Heart Is in the East* lost money on its summer run, and the extension was included in the 1983-1984 figures. The extension of *Kuni-Leml*, on the other hand, would show up the following year. As a result, the theater showed a total of $165,750 in expenses and $82,000 in earned income. The $83,750 deficit was made up, once again, through contributions and government grants.

The JRT, however, took a giant step forward in terms of subscriptions. Cohen insisted that the subscriptions doubled because of both *Kuni-Leml* and the announcement of a fall production of a play by Isaac Bashevis Singer. Actually, subscriptions had climbed rapidly from the 700 to the 900s during the 1983-1984 season, even before *Kuni-Leml* or the announcement of the Singer premiere, and, with the added impetus of those two productions, would jump to about 1500 by the fall.

Most of all, looking back over the season, *Kuni-Leml* marked a watershed for the Jewish Repertory Theatre. On the one side lay the struggling young ethnic theater, admittedly one that had grown steadily over the years, but one which identified with a small core of Jews who sought to rediscover their cultural heritage. On the other side lay a new kind of leadership and a recognition that went far beyond the borders of 14th Street.

1984-1985

The 1984-1985 season belonged to a great extent to Edward Cohen. Four out of the five plays that year were new plays, and they were either directed by Cohen or written by his playwright proteges. He directed the first and third productions—Isaac Bashevis Singer's *Shlemiel the First* and his own *City Boy*. And the last two productions of the season, Susan Sandler's *Crossing Delancey* and Nathan Gross's *Pearls*, were developed with his help. Cohen and Avni recognized that new plays were a risk at the box office, but they had great faith that both the Sandler and the Gross plays would be sure-fire attractions. As to *City Boy*, Cohen was aware that it would be controversial, but felt that the play had a statement to make and deserved to be heard.

On October 7 the theater opened the season with a "world premiere," as they called it, a new play by the renowned Nobel Laureate, Singer. The play, directed by Cohen and edited for the stage by Sarah Blacher Cohen, was Singer's off-Broadway debut.

Cohen, a frequent lecturer at seminars, had met Sarah Blacher Cohen several years earlier at a national conference on Jewish theater, held at Marymount Manhattan College. Sharing their interest, the two became friendly, and she eventually told him that she and Isaac Singer were collaborating on a play.

The play was based on several Singer short stories with the usual Singer theme of the struggle between religious and worldly passions. It takes place in a nineteenth-century Polish village and is the story of Shlemiel, a typical resident of Chelm, Yiddish folklore's legendary town of simpletons. Shlemiel is sent into the world to spread the town's "wisdom" and, on making a wrong turn, arrives in a village exactly like his own. He finds a duplicate wife and children and duplicate sages to harrass him. That is the single joke at the heart of the comedy.

Initially the plan was to present the play at the State University of New York at Albany, where Sarah Blacher Cohen taught, as part of a state-funded week-end tribute to Singer. She asked for Cohen's reactions to the play, which he gave, and he was eventually asked to direct the play at SUNY. But "through some kind of political catastrophe, this enormous budget for the commemorative Isaac Bashevis

Singer week-end at SUNY collapsed. When that happened, I suggested that we do it here.''[103] Singer agreed to the JRT production and was paid $7500 for the rights, which was "an outrageous fee, a tremendous amount of money, for the JRT,'' Cohen said, explaining that generally playwrights at the JRT are paid the standard Samuel French fee of six percent of the gross for a performance or about $600.[104]

Why did they do it?

> We knew that if we could announce a world premiere of
> a Singer play in combination with the success of *Kuni-
> Leml*, we would take a giant step in the theater—and we
> did. We doubled the subscriptions.[105]

But, subscription increase notwithstanding, *Shlemiel the First* was never the critical or popular success they expected. Only Edith Oliver had a strongly positive reaction:

> Mr. Singer has written the play with the absolute logic
> that is essential to nonsense, and the company performs
> it agreeably, under Edward Cohen's direction.[106]

Richard Shepard praised Singer as a master storyteller, but added that "in this case, he carries the joke too far, to another medium where the punch line misses the wallop it should deliver.''[107] Another critic added:

> The production falters...in its gestalt. Under Edward M.
> Cohen's directon, the inhabitants of Chelm are played
> as caricatures of fools rather than as simple silly folk.[108]

Cohen himself admitted that the play had problems from the beginning. He knew that the play was too long, and, with Singer's cooperation, cut it from twenty-six to nine characters. Cohen also wanted to cut the number of wise men from five to three and to eliminate the two children, feeling that "in a play where the whole point of view was childish and where you're going stylistically for an innocent naivete in adult characters, you don't put real childern on the stage, because real children can't play that kind of style.''[109] But Singer insisted upon retaining the children, arguing that they were needed to show Shlemiel doing something right. Ultimately, they compromised—Singer kept his children and Cohen got his three wise men. In all, however, Cohen felt that the play never worked.

> It was too long for a one-joke play. I should have cut

> more. And I don't think the audience ever really accepted
> the townspeople as charming naifs. They took them as
> stupid and they resented the play and they thought Mr.
> Singer was sneering at the characters. That was because
> we didn't hit the right tone. And the main reason, I think,
> was because we had those children....I also know that
> when you work off-Broadway, it's hard to get good child-
> ren. And they took up an enormous amount of rehear-
> sal time.[110]

The play, Cohen conceded, probably has to be done in Yiddish to
be successful, to keep its quaint tone.[111]

Shlemiel did bring David Rosenberg to the JRT for the first time
as production stage manager. Rosenberg, who had known Edward
Cohen at Playwrights Horizons in earlier years, would henceforth
be a JRT regular, as had been many others before him in other capac-
ities. Rosenberg, in fact, went on to work on three more shows that
season—*City Boy, Crossing Delancey* and *Pearls.*

As stage manager, he had his problems, among them the difficulty
of seeing the stage from the lighting booth and of admitting actors
into the locked building on Saturdays. In addition, a back door, be-
hind the seating, fitted improperly, causing flooding after rainstorms.
But thievery presented the major problem:

> The security is bad, and things are stolen out from un-
> der you. We had to remove the lighting board and wheel
> out the sound equipment on a cart after each performance.
> We put it in a vault downstairs, which is a hassle. In most
> theaters, the booth is secure and everything is perma-
> nent.[112]

But, on the positive side, Rosenberg found a small, intimate thater
and exciting plays.

> They try to do interesting plays, as most theaters do, but
> I think they succeed in their goals—in doing plays that
> appeal to the audience and also plays that challenge.[113]

Following *Shlemiel* in December was the Ronald Ribman drama
entitled *Cold Storage*, the only play of the year which did not involve
Cohen. Set in a hospital, the play deals with two cancer patients and
their nurse. Produced originally at the American Place Theater in
1977, the play moved on to Broadway, and, with Len Cariou in the

lead, won the Dramatists Guild Hall-Warriner Award for the Best Play of 1977.

Cariou, who had performed in *Up From Paradise*, was interested both in directing *Cold Storage* and in working again at the JRT, and, when he met Avni at a JRT fund-raiser, the two discussd the possibility. Avni was not sure about the play as a choice for his theater, since its connection to Jewish themes seemed dubious. But the small cast of three appealed to Avni, as did Cariou himself as a drawing card.

Avni agreed, despite his reservations. Cariou then assembled a cast headed by Joe Silver, who had been so popular in the JRT's *The Homecoming* production, along with Jay Thomas and Odalys Dominguez. Avni felt that Cariou went on to stage a strong show, but one that was, unfortunately, not a crowd-pleaser. It may have been the subject matter, which had to be depressing despite Ribman's light treatment. But Avni felt that the difficulty lay in competition from cable television:

> It was running on cable TV at the same time, three times a day, the same time we were playing. I didn't know they had filmed the play. So we didn't get the audience turn-out, except for the subscribers. It was too bad.[114]

Richard Shepard, however, praised the show as an "earful of good dialogue delivered by actors worth going to see":

> It has no real plot but always seems to be going somewhere and, even though it never does, it achieves its own sort of dynamic and makes for a lively theatrical experience.[115]

The theater's next production, *City Boy*, turned out to be the JRT's worst disaster, in terms of audience reaction. The play, which had been adapted by Cohen from a collection of author Leonard Michael's short stories, with both writers working together closely. It had been presented successfully the previous winter at the JRT as a staged reading. Cohen had long admired Michael's work and had wanted to adapt it. He had known Michaels personally. Both had grown up on Manhattan's Lower East Side and Cohen was a friend of Michael's younger brother. "We came from the same background," Cohen said. "We had the same voice. We had the same vision. There's an enormous amount of sympatico."[116]

Avni insisted that he had never liked the play, even as a staged reading, but Cohen persuaded him that such experimental plays should be staged. Plant's reaction was even stronger:

> Having read the script, he stormed into the office and said, "I never interfere, but why are you doing this horrible play?" Ed stood his ground, saying it was a good play.[117]

Cohen went on to shape the staged readng into a full-scale production and to direct it.

The play deals with Myron, a New York Jewish boy and his blonde Gentile wife from Minnesota, who meet, marry and part through a series of vignettes. Also involved in the drama is Myron's friend Ickstein, a poet and homosexual who lives in the same apartment building.

Attendance proved to be low; at about 1500, it was the lowest that season. Nevertheless, the faithful subscribers showed up, as they did to every JRT show. Unfortunately, many of them departed midway through the play, noisily voicing their disapproval, objecting to the obscenities, the circumstances and, most of all, the portrayal of young Jews as homosexuals and failures. Not only did they find the subject matter offensive, but they found the theme and plot confusing.

Reviewers also reacted negatively. Herbert Mitgang said:

> The tipoff...is that no playwright is listed in the playbill.... "City Boy" is really a reading disguised as a play, more suitable for a rainy night at the Poetry Center of the 92nd Street Y. If love and marriage have only Myrons out there in Manhattan, that blonde should never have left St. Cloud.[118]

The April production, also an original play with much Cohen input, had a totally opposite effect on JRT audiences and reviewers. Avni suspected, from early rehearsals on, that it would be a solid success, and he was right.

The play was *Crossing Delancey*, written by actress-playwright Susan Sandler. Sandler was one of Cohen's playwrights-in-residence (see Chapter 5), and she worked closely with him throughout the play's development, from its staged reading earlier in the season to its final presentation.

Crossing Delancey had a sure-fire appeal to the tradition-minded

JRT audiences, perhaps because the play itself was traditional in values. It was a warm, loving story of a Jewish girl who makes the choice between two suitors—one a writer of the pretentious, sophisticated, uptown literary world and the other a "pickle man," a Jewish entrepreneur from the Lower East Side. Central to the story is the heroine's *Bubbie*,[119] who provides wisdom, sanity and love in equal doses.

Pamela Berlin, a director with considerable background at the Ensemble Studio Theater and other New York and regional theaters, had directed the staged reading and went on to do the show itself. Berlin cast Melanie Mayron in the lead, an actress with solid credentials in both films and live theater. The other four in the cast—Sylvia Kauders, Shirley Stoler, Geoffrey Pierson and Jacob Harran, were all seasoned performers. The set designer Jeffrey Schneider, by this time a veteran of the JRT, created a simple but ingenious set that encompassed three locales successfully on the small stage.

Audiences responded warmly, spreading the word among friends, and the turnout (with an attendance of 2778) was considerably better than the two previous shows.

Critics were equally enthusiastic. Most praised the show with such adjectives as heart-warming, winning, bubbly, zesty, and they praised the actors, directors, playwright, and set designer equally. Elenore Lester pointed out that "playwright Susan Sandler has a gift for satire, an ear for dialogue, feeling for character and a good grasp of the sociological scene."[120] Millicent Brower said that Sandler had accomplished the impossible: "Her play...is a satisfying modern comedy about a very old theme: matchmaking....The Jewish Repertory Theatre...has given us another hit."[121] Richard Shepard was more reserved in his praise:

> "Crossing Delancey" is not so much a full play as it is an enacted short story, or interacting vignettes that have fresh characters, a simple, even predictable, plot and a feeling for romantic verities...."Crossing Delancey" tells its unpretentious story believably, rarely trying to make its gag lines... upstage its narration or outshine its heart. Flawed it may be but somehow that doesn't seem to affect it as a nice theater diversion.[122]

Cohen's assessment of Sandler as a commercial writer and her play's commercial potential was right. After the JRT production, the show was optioned for a commercial New York production and Sandler was then asked by Joan Micklin Silver to turn the play into a film script.

The theater's final show of the season was a new musical that could be classified as more opera than popular musical. Entitled *Pearls*, it was written by Nathan Gross (book, music and lyrics) and starred the noted opera singer Rosalind Elias. For the first time the JRT departed from its usual procedure of equal billing for all actors, and featured the star's name above the title.

Nathan Gross was a Cohen discovery. Gross had sent Cohen a script of a one-woman show called *Ida*. Cohen did not like the play but recognized Gross's potential as a lyricist. He continued to encourage him, and Gross's next offering was a musical about an upper West Side psychotherapist, which Cohen felt was not right for the JRT. But Cohen became really excited when he discovered that Gross could translate Yiddish, and urged him to do something drawing on Yiddish literature.

As a result Gross turned to *Mirele Efros*, a powerful 1898 drama by Yiddish playwright Jacob Gordin, and within a few weeks he had brought in the first act of his new musical. Both Avni and Cohen found the music beautiful.

The play itself, often called *The Jewish Queen Lear*, was the story of a rich, domineering woman who devotes herself totally to a weak son. Conflict and tragedy arise when the son marries a young, independent and equally strong woman. In Yiddish theater, the drama provided a rich role for the theater's most famous actresses, with Ida Kaminska, the star of the Yiddish stage, performing it in Poland and New York.

Gross's musical was slated for a June opening, with Avni directing. As Avni began to seek a lead for the role of Mirele, he looked for an older woman, a singer-actress with a marvelous voice. His first thought was Roberta Peters, but she refused the role, and he then approached Rosalind Elias, a mezzo-soprano who had performed with the Metropolitan Opera and other opera companies throughout the world:

> We sent her the script, which she liked, and we had a
> meeting in her apartment, where Gross played the music.

I fell in love with her. I thought she was sensational. And she really wanted to to the show, if we could work out the dates with her agent.[123]

The show opened at the end of June and ran through the month of July. Many JRT regulars were involved in the production: actors Richard Frisch and Grace Roberts, set designer Jeffrey Schneider, costume designer Karen Hummel, choreographer Haila Straus, and production stage manager David Rosenberg.

Undoubtedly because of the stature of the production's star and the growing reputation of the JRT, the show was thoroughly reviewed by large and small New York papers, the suburban press and the Jewish press. Critics had mixed reactions to the musical, with some finding it impressive, fresh and zesty and others seeing it as dated. But all were in strong agreement about mezzo-soprano Elias, seeing her performance as towering. Elenore Lester said:

Rosalind Elias... brings her own kind of distinction to this updated version of "Mirele Efros." Her powerful voice is matched by a powerful presence.[124]

And Marilyn Stasio agreed:

Metropolitan Opera star Rosalind Elias makes an impressive figure of the matriarch, her regal mezzo delineating whatever character shadings may elude her as an actress.[125]

With the season's end, the Jewish Rep for Young Audiences, which had been operating for three and a half years, was quietly dropped. "We just didn't have enough money to continue paying a salary and the travelling expenses, taking the shows to schools and community centers, nor did we have the space here, " said Geller.[126]

The 1984-1985 season, in all, was artistically a mixed experience for the JRT. On the positive side, the JRT had dared to take risks, mounting four new shows in one season, a courageous and commendable move for any theater. But it was also a dangerous move, and, in fact, audiences responded badly to two of the new plays. Even the successes, *Crossing Delancey* and *Pearls*, were not of the dimension of *Kuni-Leml* or *Vagabond Stars*.

Financially, while tickets sales had increased, expenses had also mounted. In preparing an NEA grant application, Don Geller indicated that the total JRT expenses for the 1984-1985 season were

$323,373, as compared to the previous year's expenses of $220,803. Earned income from all sources, Geller claimed, was $207,357, a clear improvement over the previous year's $97,992. Nevertheless, the gap between earnings and expenses remained about the same— about $121,000 for 1984-1985 compared to the previous year's $122,000. That gap was met, as in the previous year, by $28,000 in funding, $27,000 from the Y Board and fund-raising events, and $45,000 from other contributors.

In all, the 1980s saw the JRT become a substantial company, taking its place in the forefront of ethnic and off-Broadway theaters. The JRT moved from showcase contracts, with unpaid personnel, up the Equity ladder to mini-contract, where actors received weekly wages for rehearsals and performances. The theater's ticket sales catapulted upward between 1980 and 1985, showing a total gate of $32,000 in June 1980, compared to a total gate of $194,000 in June 1985 (which, granted, did include $76,000 for the extended summer run of *Kuni-Leml*). Subscription figures jumped from something under 700 in the early 1980s to 1500 by 1985; though the JRT had defectors from time to time, it built a consistently loyal following. Moreover, the audience expanded to draw on, not only the neighborhood, but the New York City boroughs and the suburbs. And the theater came to be one of the few off-Broadway or ethnic theaters reviewed steadily by major New York newspapers.

As the theater grew in size and sophistication, it grew, like all nonprofit theaters, in expenditures, which were never covered by its earned income. This was a constant headache for Don Geller, who had, in effect, created a Frankenstein. Why did he, under the circumstances, continue to sponsor the theater?

> It is a good question, one that I've pondered. But the fact
> is that the theater continues to meet the original goals we
> had promulgated as being significant for the Y. It has done
> so all along. Now the only issue for us is, indeed, how
> do we support and maintain it, and I think it's important
> that we do so. [127]

Several newcomers in the 1980s began to work regularly with the company and did much to enhance its reputation: composer Raphael Crystal and writer Nahma Sandrow (who were involved in the company's greatest successes), set designer Jeffrey Schneider, and director Anthony McKay, were perhaps the most important. Moreover, well-known professionals were happy to work at the JRT, and stars such as Len Cariou and Joe Silver and Austin Pendleton began to appear on the roster.

The 1980s saw the launching of Edward Cohen's Playwrights-in-Residence program, stemming from a $10,000 National Endowment for the Arts grant. Cohen would help his playwrights to fine-tune and develop works, many of which were presented in staged readings series and full productions, both at the JRT and elsewhere. He also continued to examine numerous scripts and work with the writers outside the Playwrights-in-Residence program.

Not every major production of the 1980s followed a magic formula, and the JRT had its triumphs and its disasters. The highlights included: Arthur Miller's *Incident at Vichy*, produced in June 1981 and directed by Avni himself; Clifford Odets's *Awake and Sing!* (October 1981), directed by Lynn Polan, the musical *Vagabond Stars* (June 1982), which launched the Sandrow-Crystal-Avni team, and, above all, their later musical, the enormously successful *Kuni-Leml* (June 1984).

The successes were interspersed with many less memorable productions and with some outright disasters. The production of Isaac Singer's *Shlemiel the First* was a disappointment to both critics and audiences. And *Escape from Riverdale*, by Don Wollner, one of Cohen's PIRs, played in April 1984 to very hostile audiences. The JRT's older, conservative viewers had little use for a play that depicted a young, hip scene complete with sexual encounters and verbal obscenities. Cohen's own play, *City Boy*, presented in February 1985, was more of the same, as far as JRT audiences were concerned, and many viewers left midway through the performance.

Yet the JRT weathered such experiences. In all, the JRT had clearly established itself as a respected, noted off-Broadway theater, so much so that it could take risks and present new work that its audiences might not always like. Invariably, the solidly popular plays drew the audiences back. But, more importantly, theatergoers kept coming back because they wanted to support and to be involved with Jewish theater, particularly good Jewish theater. And the JRT, they believed, was providing just that.

[1]Ran Avni, interview, New York City, 19 July 1985.
[2]Ibid.
[3]Ibid.
[4]Richard F. Shepard, "Theater: Gertrude Berg's 'Me and Molly,'" *New York Times*, 31 October 1980.
[5]Michael Albert Mantel, interview, New York City, 28 May 1985.
[6]Ibid.
[7]Jeffrey Schneider, interview, New York City, 10 June 1985.
[8]A Yiddish term meaning "guts" or gizzards.
[9]Mantel, interview, 28 May 1985.
[10]Richard F. Shepard, "Evil and the System," *New York Times*, 23 December 1980.
[11]Anthony McKay, interview, Westport, Connecticut, 30 December 1985.
[12]Ibid.
[13]Ibid.
[14]Ibid.
[15]A Yiddish word, meaning "craziness" or "nonsense."
[16]McKay, interview, 30 December 1985.
[17]Ibid.
[18]John S. Patterson, "Pinter's Comedy of Menace: Worth Doing?" *Villager*, February 1981.
[19]Jennifer Dunning, "Stage: Jewish Repertory In Pinter's 'Birthday Party,'" *New York Times*, 20 February 1981.
[20]Avni, interview, 19 July 1985.
[21]Ibid.
[22]Ibid.
[23]Shepard, "Stage: Jewish Rep's 'Indicent at Vichy,'" *New York Times*, 12 June 1981.
[24]Avni, interview, 19 July 1985.
[25]Ibid.
[26]Shepard, *New York Times*, 12 June 1981.
[27]Joseph Hurley, "Mixed Intentions," *Soho News*, 29 September 1981.
[28]Avni, interview, 14 September 1985.
[29]Ibid.
[30]Mantel, interview, 28 May 1985.
[31]Polan, interview, 5 April, 1985.
[32]Richard F. Shepard, "Stage: Odets's 'Awake and Sing!'," *New York Times*, 1 November 1981.
[33]Deborah Hart Strober, "Odets revival a period piece of pre-Hitler nostalgia," *Jewish Week-American Examiner*, 8 November 1981.

[34]Mel Gussow, "Stage: Rush's 'Elephants' By the Jewish Repertory," *New York Times*, 22 December 1981.

[35]J. Peter Brunswick, "Harsh Realities of Urban Experience on Stage," *Long Island Jewish World*, 25 December 1981.

[36]Debbi Wasserman, "Opposite Attractions," *Other Stages*, 17 December 1981.

[37]Avni, interview, 14 September 1985.

[38]Joseph Hurley, "A Dream and an Omen," *Other Stages*, 11 February 1982.

[39]Elenore Lester, "Rarely performed, Delmore Schwartz play offers insight into family life," *Jewish Week-American Examiner*, 28 February 1982.

[40]Avni, interview, 14 September 1985.

[41]Ibid.

[42]Howard Waxman, "Pantagleize: European Classic on Stage," *Jewish World/Long Island Jewish Press*, 7-13 May 1982.

[43]Avni, interview, 14 September 1985.

[44]Avni, interview, 14 September 1985. Avni claimed that his original idea of presenting the immigrant story in chronological order, with songs and skits, was later stolen by the producers of *The Golden Land*. *The Golden Land* had a long, successful run in 1985 at New York's Second Avenue Theatre.

[45]Raphael Crystal, interview, New York City, 14 March 1986.

[46]Richard F. Shepard, "Musical: Jewish Group With 'Vagabond Stars,'" *New York Times*, 6 June 1982.

[47]Patricia O'Haire, "Warming to the immigrant experience," *Daily News*, 12 June 1982.

[48]Marilyn Stasio, "Life as a Greenhorn," *New York Post*, 14 June 1982.

[49]Richard Laermer, "'Vagabond Stars' By The Jewish Repertory," *Arts Weekly*, 8-15 September 1982.

[50]Martin Davidson, "Time Out," *Jewish Press*, 27 August 1982.

[51]Don Geller, interview, New York City, 4 December 1985.

[52]Avni, interview, 14 September 1985.

[53]Avni was not snobbish about Shroder's community theater, as opposed to professional experience, and had in fact launched other directors who had had little prior professional experience—among them, actors Lynn Polan and Michael Mantel.

[54]Ibid.

[55]Ibid.

[56]Ibid.

[57]Laurie Stone, "Fallout," *Village Voice*, 2 November 1982.

[58]Avni was pleased that he had given Shroder the opportunity, because it was not to be repeated. Although Shroder managed to do several more shows in Florida, it was just two years later that he died of cancer.

[59]Avni, interview, 4 December 1985.

[60]Richard F. Shepard, "Theater: A Comedy, 'Friends Too Numerous,'" *New York Times*, 19 December 1982.

[61]Marilyn Stasio, "'Friends' funny enough for TV," *New York Post*, 21 December 1982.

[62]Avni, interview, 4 December 1985.

[63]McKay, interview, 30 December 1985.

[64]Millicent Brower, "The theater," *Town and Village*, 24 February 1983.

[65]Irene Backalenick, "Ivanov," *Other Stages*, 10 February 1983. At that time I was reviewing for *Other Stages*. It was my first meeting with both the theater and that Chekhov play, and I became intrigued with both, questioning why the play had been performed at a so-called Jewish theater and its significance in Jewish terms. This interest ultimately led to a choice of the theater as a dissertation topic.

[66]Avni, interview, 4 December 1985.

[67]Richard F. Shepard, "Stage: 'Taking Steam,' Life on the Sunset Side," 24 April 1983.

[68]The Sephardim are descendants of Jews who lived in Spain and Portugal until the 15th century and then resettled in Mediterranean lands, bringing their own customs and the Ladino language (a mix of Hebrew and Spanish). Today the term is used to mean Jews from Arab lands and they comprise 50 percent of the Jews in Israel. The Ashkenazim, on the other hand, are the Jews who lived in Germany in the Middle Ages, moved gradually into eastern Europe, carrying heir own language (Yiddish), and eventually providing the main reservoir of Jewish immigration to the United States.

[69]Avni, interview, 4 December 1985.

[70]Richard F. Shepard, "Stage: Jewish Rep Musical About Sephardic Poet," *New York Times*, 19 June 1983.

[71]Marilyn Stasio, "Halevy play, full of 'Heart,' " *New York Post*, 4 July 1983.

[72]Avni, interview, 4 December 1985.

[73]Alfred Plant, letter to JRT subscribers, September 1983.

[74]Ibid.

[75]Ibid.

[76]Ibid.

[77]Frank Rich, "Stage: Miller's 'Up From Paradise,' " *New York Times*, 26 October 1983.

[78]John Simon, *New York Magazine*, 7 November 1983.

[79]Edith Oliver, "Musical Beginning," *New Yorker*, 7 November 1983.

[80]John Beaufort, " 'Up From Paradise': biblical themes in contemporary dress," *Christian Science Monitor*, 3 November 1983.

[81]Linda Winer, "Miller's 'Paradise' is relaxed, hip fun," *USA Today*, 26 October 1983.

[82]Avni, interview, 4 December 1985.

[83]Frank Rich, "Stage: 'Gifted Children,' " *New York Times*, 23 December 1983.

[84]Avni, interview, 4 December 1985. *Meshugenah* is a Yiddish expression, translated as "a crazy person."

[85]Don Nelsen, " 'Gifted Children' harmed by mother," *Daily News*, 7 December 1983.

[86]Avni, interview, 4 December 1985.

[87]Avni, interview, 28 July 1986.

[88]Lillie Rosen, " 'The Homecoming' Proves To Be Unusual Family Affair," *Jewish Journal*, 16 March 1983.

[89]Herbert Mitgang, "Theater: Revival of 'Homecoming,' " *New York Times*, 24 February 1984.

[90]Richard F. Shepard, "Theater: 'Riverdale,' By Jewish Repertory," *New York Times*, 24 April 1984.

[91]Avni, interview, 4 December 1985.

[92]The name "Kuni-Leml" has come to signify, in Yiddish, a simpleton, and the word is used interchangeably.

[93]Avni, interview, 4 December 1985.

[94]Ibid.

[95]Richard F. Shepard, "Theater: 'Kuni-Leml,' Adapted From Yiddish," *New York Times*, 16 June 1984.

[96]Laurie Stone, "Between Two Worlds," *Village Voice*, 3 July 1984.

[97]Leora Mann, "A Fable in Fool's Disguise at Jewish Rep," *Villager Downtown*, 28 June 1984.

[98]Avni, interview, 17 December 1985.

[99]Mel Gussow, "Critic's Notebook," *New York Times*, 31 October 1984.

[100]Marilyn Stasio, "Yiddish oldie as musical," *New York Post*, 17 October 1984.

[101]Madd., "Kuni-Leml," *Variety*, 31 October 1984.

[102]Otis L. Guernsey Jr., ed., *The Burns Mantle Yearbook, The Best Plays of 1984-1985* (New York: Dodd, Mead & Co., 1985), p. 19.

[103]Edward Cohen, interview, New York City, 17 February 1986.

[104]Ibid.

[105]Ibid.

[106]Edith Oliver, "Off Broadway," *New Yorker*, 5 November 1984.

[107]Richard F. Shepard, "Theater: A Singer Play, 'Shlemiel the First,' " *New York Times*, 26 October 1984.

[108]Leora Manischewitz, "Theater: This Singer Isn't Quite First-Rate Theater," *Villager Downtown*, 24 October 1984.

[109]Cohen, interview, 17 February 1986.

[110]Ibid.

[111]The play was performed in Yiddish in the fall of 1986 in Canada and did prove to be highly successful.

[112]David Rosenberg, interview, New York City, 22 July 1985.

[113]Ibid.

[114]Avni, interview, 17 December 1985.

[115]Richard F. Shepard, "Stage: 'Cold Storage,' " *New York Times*, 16 December 1984.

[116]Samuel Freedman, "Two Authors Venture Into Alien Land of Theater," *New York Times*, 8 February 1985.

[117]Avni, interview, 17 December 1985.

[118]Herbert Mitgang, "Stage: Jewish Repertory Offers 'City Boy,' " *New York Times*, 17 February 1985.

[119]The Yiddish word for grandmother.

[120]Elenore Lester, "This zesty comedy is bubbly because of Bubbie," *Jewish Week*, 17 May 1985.

[121]Millicent Brower, "A triumph in modern match making," *Town and Village*, 2 May 1985.

[122]Richard F. Shepard, "The Theater: 'Crossing Delancey,' " *New York Times*, 2 May 1985.

[123]Avni, interview, 17 December 1985.

[124]Elenore Lester, " 'Pearls,' oldtime Yiddish hit, updated as zesty musical comedy," *Jewish Week*, 19 July 1985.

[125]Marilyn Stasio, "Dark opera from a Yiddish classic," *New York Post*, 17 July 1985.

[126]Don Geller, interview, New York City, 16 September 1986.

[127]Ibid.

CHAPTER

5

The Playwrights-In-Residence Program

The 1982-1983 season marked a turning point in the development of the Jewish Repertory Theatre. In September of that year Edward Cohen, JRT's literary manager, called a historic meeting, bringing together five young Jewish playwrights—Dan Ellentuck, Donald Margulies, Susan Sandler, Micahel Taav, and Don Wollner.

Cohen had just received a National Endowment for the Arts grant, placing him for the first time on a sound financial footing at the JRT. "Until then," Cohen said, "I had been paid in bits and pieces, very little money, and my obligation was merely to do playreadings and find plays for the JRT."[1] But the $10,000 grant for a director fellowship gave Cohen the opportunity to work solidly at the theater and to develop new programs. His immediate plan was to launch a playwrights-in-residence program.

Cohen claimed that there was a double reason to find and help develop young Jewish playwrights. First of all, the JRT, as he saw it, was a living theater; therefore, it should not restrict itself to presenting only older plays of Jewish content or revivals and classics. There was a need for contemporary statements about the Jewish experience, and these young playwrights were ideally suited to such a task. Secondly, Cohen believed that someone should force these dramatists to confront their Jewish identity and to acknowledge it openly in their work.

Citing Don Wollner's *Badgers*, a play about college undergraduates, as an example, Cohen says,

> He had never seen himself as a Jewish writer. I told him,
> "That's what you have to deal with in this play. These
> are Jewish kids." He didn't know that. When he made
> those kids clearly Jewish, the play had a new vitality. And
> the next play was clearly about Jewish kids. [2]

In creating the program, Cohen sought out writers who were already on their way. "I wanted writers who had reached a certain level of professional achievement," he explained. "I did not want students or neophytes." [3] Moreover, he turned to playwrights whose work he knew and who had had strong connections with the JRT.

Donald Margulies, for example, had partcipated the previous season in a full-scale production entitled *Delmore*, based on the life of the poet, Delmore Schwartz. The same season saw staged readings of Susan Sandler's *Companion Pieces*, Michael Taav's *Movie Love* and Don Wollner's *Rookies*. The year before Wollner's *Badgers* had been read, and in the 1979-1980 season both Margulies's *Luna Park* and Dan Ellentuck's *Fat Fell Down* were read. Later several of these plays were given full-scale productions, either at the JRT or other off-Broadway theaters, such as the Ensemble Studio Theater or the Manhattan Punch Line. The playwrights were, as Cohen saw them, young people of considerable promise and potential.

Cohen approached the program with an open mind, with the idea that the playwrights themselves would give it content and direction. It was fortunate that he had a low-keyed approach. The playwrights arrived at the meeting with a good deal of wariness. "Several of them had questions about connecting with the JRT," said Cohen. "it's not the most commercial thing you can do in your life, admitting the

Jewish connection.''[4]

Professionals who took their work seriously, the playwrights were not at all sure that they needed one more activity. Time was a precious commodity. What was Ed Cohen offering? Was he talking about a stipend, such as other wealthier theaters offered playwrights? Would they be co-opted? Would they be locked into an exlusive arrangement that would close out other opportunities? Would they be forced to write only Jewish plays? Was he setting up a playwrights-in-residence program to justify a grant application for the JRT? Would they be obliged to attend meetings, listening to pointless speeches? What was in it for them?

Susan Sandler indicated,

> If one is a playwright-in-residence at Milwaukee Rep, that means the company supports you for that season to the tune of $20,000, so we had a heated discussion along those lines. Are we being given anything for the use of our names in this project, or are we simply a means to an end for a grant proposal to you? That was what it felt like at first.[5]

Cohen explained that the theater had no money to give them, but it could offer support in the form of staged readings and personal feedback. He would work closely with them in developing scripts, an area in which he had experience and expertise. Moreover, it would be a lifetime membership, not the typical temporary arrangement of theaters and playwrights. The JRT would not exert undue pressure to produce commercially viable material. At the same time the title itself, ''playwright-in-residence.'' would lend prestige both to the playwright and to the theater, according to Cohen, as each continued to grow in recognition and status. It would be a mutual support system.

Cohen never envisaged a formally structured program, with a large membership and regular meetings. He wanted to keep it small, personal and informal. He explains,

> I was a member of a playwrights' group for seven years, a highly structured organization. And what happened was that all the no-talents, the losers, came to the meetings and did all the work, while the really talented people were just too busy. What happens when you do that is that the

people who have nothing else to do attend the meetings
and end up running the organization. I didn't want that.[6]
Nevertheless, Cohen believed that the playwrights themselves should
be allowed to determine the ultimate format. The program could take
any form they wished, with considerable or limited contact with each
other, with a formal or informal framework.

It was a difficult meeting in many respects. As part of the session,
Michael Taav read a play of his that was in progress at the time. "It
was a disaster," Cohen recalled. "It was a difficult play that the other
playwrights apparently didn't understand, and they sat stony-faced
through Michael's reading, which wasn't the best reading."[7] But
several playwrights had a different recollection, with both Sandler
and Ellentuck recalling how impressed they were with Taav's work.
The problems may have stemmed from other factors, such as the setting. With little available space at the busy YMHA, with its innumerable classes and workshops, the playwrights were confined to the
JRT's small dressing room. A second meeting, Don Wollner remembers, was held in the nursery room, where they discussed the future
of Jewish theater sitting in tiny seats.

A greater problem was the reaction to Ran Avni's welcoming
speech, as Wollner describes it,

> It was a strange discourse in which he said, "I suppose
> we have to have the new writers." It was phrased in the
> most inappropriate language. I think we were all alienated
> and disembodied and depressed by the circumstances.
> And understandably, it was the worst possible audience
> for Michael Taav.[8]

Sandler felt that something firm should be offered to the playwrights
and suggested that the JRT present a series of their one-act plays,
similar to the Ensemble Studio Theater's playwright series, *Mara-
thon*. Despite a heated discussion, with Ran Avni on one side, the
playwrights on the other, and Cohen in the middle, the proposal was
rejected. Avni, with the final veto, saw it as an unnecessary risk, i.e.,
as a project that would not appeal to his audiences.

But within that first meeting, questions were thrashed out, accomo-
dations were reached, and the playwrights-in-residence program was
born. Cohen summarizes,

> You could sense, despite the fiery misery of that first

meeting, that something important was happening to them. I think it was in terms of the Jewishness. One of them said, ''What are you telling us about Jewish writing? We are all here. We're Jewish. This is the JRT. That's enough!'' I agreed.[9]

In the two years following the 1982 meeting two more PIRs were added: Richard Schotter and Nahma Sandrow. Schotter's play *Benya the King* was given a staged reading in the 1978-1979 season and a full-scale production in December 1979. Nahma Sandrow translated and adapted Yiddish writings to create *Vagabond Stars*, produced at the JRT in June 1982. She followed her first effort two years later with *Kuni-Leml*, an adaptation of Avrom Goldfadn's Yiddish show, a musical that would prove to be JRT's biggest commercial success.

The seven PIRs, though markedly different in many respects, share characteristics. The five men and two women are all based in New York City, all in their thirties and forties, all Jewish, all with work produced on stage, and all with an appreciation for Ed Cohen's role in their development. Most were born in New York City, and their work bears the stamp of the city. Similar themes emerge in their plays: alienation, separation and loss, and oppression.[10]

But there are clearly two sub-groups. On the one hand, there are the two academicians—Richard Schotter and Nahma Sandrow. Both are in their fourties, both are married and have children. Both teach full-time within the City University of New York college system. As playwrights, both have focused on adaptations, drawing on material from the Jewish past. Although Schotter has written several original pieces and considers himself a playwright, his greatest recognition as a playwright has come from *Benya the King*, based on the work of a Yiddish writer and dealing with an Eastern European milieu. Sandrow sees herself as teacher and historian, a writer of books, with her role in theater limited to that of adapter and translator.

The other five, all younger (in their 30s), are primarily playwrights, although they support themselves in a variety of ways. Their work is original, often sharply satirical, and focuses on the contemporary social scene and their own life experiences. Let us turn to the first of these playwrights.

DONALD MARGULIES

Of the seven, only Donald Margulies has succeeded in supporting himself full-time as a playwright. He had been enormously productive since college graduation in 1977, with a total literary output that now includes some twenty plays and other projects for theater, film and television. He has gained steadily in recognition, as his work has appeared in all media. His plays have had both staged readings and full productions at the JRT and numerous other off-off-Broadway theaters.

Awards have included a 1984 New York State CAPS (Creative Artists Public Service) Grant and 1984 and 1985 Sundance Institute Summer Fellowships for *What's Wrong With This Picture?*—a black comedy about death (called "brilliant by Edward Cohen) which was produced in January 1985 by the Manhattan Theater Club. (Because of the author's dissatisfaction with the production, critics were not invited.)

Margulies has been a national finalist twice in the Berman Playwriting Award (sponsored by the National Foundation for Jewish Culture for new plays of Jewish interest)—for *Pals* in 1981 and *Found a Peanut* in 1983. *Found a Peanut*, which had had readings at the WPA Theater and the Circle Repertory Company, was produced by Joseph Papp for the New York Shakespeare Festival in May 1984. *Luna Park* was named one of the best plays of 1982 by the newpaper *Other Stages*.

Other Margulies plays include: *Resting Place*, produced at the Thater for the New City in April 1982; *Tuna on Rye and Other Short Pieces*, presented at the Ensemble Studio Theater's 1983 Octoberfest; *Gifted Children* at the JRT in November 1983; *Ain't Nobody's Business*, a one-act play commissioned by Actors Theater of Louisville in 1984; *Zimmer* at the JRT in 1987. (*The Model Apartment*, his latest play, about the child of Holocaust survivors and her parents, has been optioned by Mr. Papp.)

Margulies's screen scripts include: *The Autograph Hound*, commissioned by Stiller and Meara Enterprises and based on a novel by John Lahr, as well as *Honeymoon*, an origianl romantic comedy. (He is currently working on a screen play.)

For television Margulies has written an ABC Afterschool Special and dramatic episodes. A comedy series, set in the 1960s, is in development with Disney Studios. Under commission by Norman Lear's Embassy Television to develop comedy shows, Margulies wrote a comedy pilot entitled *Danny*, which dealt with the life of the contemporary young single male and his relationships with today's independent, career-oriented women.

Margulies is perhaps the prototype of the JRT's playwright-in-residence—a young, Jewish, college-educated New Yorker. Raised in Brooklyn, he attended New York public schools. Showing early talent in the arts, he was encouraged in that area and indeed went on to a BFA degree in visual arts at the State University of New York at Purchase. At the same time, in his undergraduate years, his interest in writing flowered and found expression in playwrighting, under the tutelage of theater critic/historian Julius Novick, a SUNY professor. Margulies says that he met the right person at the right time, at a time when he was eager to write. In short order he wrote four one-act plays.

At SUNY Margulies and his fellow students formed a rudimentary group, he says, called the Playwrights Workshop Theater. His play *The Waiting Room*—"a very arch little thing which has its moments, but not anything I would want to see again"—provided his first live theater experience.[11] It proved to be a life-changing experience, determining his later choice of career.

But upon graduation he found work in New York as a book and graphic designer (work that he would pursue for three years, until he began to earn money as a writer). He also enrolled in a Master of Fine Arts program in creative writing at Brooklyn College. He soon left the program and, through Julius Novick, made contact with Jeffrey Sweet, then literary manager of an off-off-Broadway theater called The Encompass. At the time Sweet was forming a writers' group, which ultimately became the New York Writers' Bloc. Launched in October 1978, the group included actors, directors, writers. In short order, it proved to be a dynamic workshop for plays in progress. Margulies described it as a supportive and critical group, a group that provided his "major education" in playwrighting. "All the plays I've written since 1978—*Luna Park, Gifted Children, Found a Peanut, What's Wrong with this Picture?, The Model Apartment, Zimmer*—got started at the Writers' Bloc or were worked on there.''[12] Describing the dynamics of the Writers' Bloc, Margulies says that the Writers' Bloc worked, that the chemistry seemed just right.

> We likened ourselves to the Living Theater in its hey-
> day. It was a good bunch of people. It still is, although
> many of us are succeeding, and success is taking us out
> of the group.[13]

Margulies first connected with the JRT, as did the other PIRs, through Cohen. Their association began in the late '70s, when Cohen was reading plays at Playwrights Horizons and stumbled across *Pals*. "He was clearly a talented writer. You could see it was there," Cohen recalls. "I wanted them to do the play at Playwrights Horizons, but they didn't."[14]

But later, at the JRT, Cohen would remember Margulies and pull him into the theater. In 1979 Cohen was approached by actress Florence Stanley to do a production of the poet Delmore Schwartz's *Shenandoah*, a play which had never been produced. Cohen was intrigued. A short play, it called for a companion piece, possibly an adaptation of a Schwartz story. Cohen called Margulies, asking him to meet with Stanley and himself. "When a young writer had someone call to say he is good, it is the greatest thing in the world. It was exciting to get that voice from the real world!" Margulies recalls.[15] The three met, and the plan took shape. Margulies began an adaptation of Schwartz's best-known short story, "In Dreams Begin Responsibilities." Taking it through three drafts, Margulies found that the work became his own in the process, translated into his own voice and concerns. Ultimately Margulies had a brand new forty-five-minute play, which he called *Luna Park*. Given a staged reading at the JRT in the 1979-80 season, the play was then paired with *Shanandoah* under the umbrella title of *Delmore* and produced in February 1982. It was Margulies's first production in New York and his first with JRT.

Luna Park is based on Schwartz's story of a dream about his parents' courtship, a dream that he had on his twenty-first birthday. Margulies explains,

> The dream proceeds like a silent movie, reaching a cli-
> max when his father proposes to his mother, and he
> shouts, "Don't do it!" and is carted away....I opened

it up and created a context for the dream. Rather than spectator, Schwartz becomes participant, a recurring character, in the various events during the day.[16]

In December 1983 Margulies' play *Gifted Children* was staged at the JRT. The production had mixed reviews, which came down hard on the performers. The lead actress Zohra Lampert, reviewers felt, displayed an exaggerated style which seemed better suited to television and film, the areas where she has had most success. Moreover, the play, a statement of the 1980s, struck few responsive chords in JRT's audience of older, traditionally-minded people.

Despite such problems, Margulies maintains a loyalty toward and identity with the JRT. Does he see himself, then, as a ''Jewish playwright''? The answer is complicated,

> I see myself as a playwright who is invariably writing from his experience. And my experience is that of a Jew growing up in an urban environment in the '60s through the '80s. To categorize me as a Jewish playwright is kind of beside the point.[17]

The implication is that Jewishness is part of his experience, but not the total experience.

> I certainly don't shirk the association. Just as I am a member of the Dramatists' Guild, which identifies me as a dramatist, being a playwright-in-residence at the JRT identifies me as a Jewish playwright. But to say merely that I am a Jewish playwright, or that I am a playwright who writes only about Jewish themes, is not accurate. I write about themes which are, I hope, humanistic, but specifically, in many cases, Jewish. Some one has said, ''in the specific is the universal.'' And I believe that.[18]

The Jewish roots are not to be denied.

> I have a theory that for all of us, our childhoods are inescapable, that as far away as we go and no matter what we learn, we are still the same people, surrounded by the same values that we are either breaking out against or trying to make sense of. So in that respect I am a Jewish playwright.[19]

He was aware of his Jewish identity at an early age. He attended a Yiddish school for a year at age eight, enabling him, for example, to converse with his grandparents. Later he attended Hebrew school, conducted primarily in English, but the Yiddish was not forgotten.

> I've retained a lot of the idiomatic expressions and it's become part of my vocabulary. The way that I perceive speech, I think, is inherently Jewish. The rhythms that were established all the years that I was listening are indelible.[20]

The humanistic and universal themes with which Margulies deals are those of separation, loss and the ephemeral nature of friendship, played out against the backdrop of twentieth-century urban America. Nowhere are the themes examined more effectively than in Margulies's *Found a Peanut*, a tale of Jewish children who are Brooklyn apartment house dwellers. Interpersonal relationships are devoid of adult pretense and are examined from the vivid, starkly honest view of the child. Within that child's world, Margulies' outsider struggles to gain acceptance.

Margulies' work, like that of any serious playwright, has grown out of his total experiences, those of childhood as well as adulthood. His special ability to analyze, utilize and express those experiences, to weld the past with the present, the Jewish with the non-Jewish, makes him a prime and successful example of today's young Jewish-American writer.

DON WOLLNER

Similar themes appear in the work of Margulies's fellow playwrights-in-residence. Don Wollner, for instance, describes his dominant theme as the struggle of the outsider, and his characters, too, are tortured by self-doubts and a lack of peer acceptance. *A Date with Candy* portrays a young girl who uses promiscuity to counteract her loneliness and buy her way into group acceptance. Wollner's play, produced at the JRT in 1983 with another of his one-act plays, *White Devils*, under the blanket title of *Escape from Riverdale*, suffered a fate similar to Margulies's *Gifted Children*. Again, the play was too shocking, too controversial, too contemporary, for JRT audiences.

Leaving the theater, theatergoers were heard to comment, Wollner himself says,

> "The '60s are over. Why do I have to sit here for this?"

"It's real, it's dramatic, I don't want it!" "I don't need
to pay $14 for this. I can talk to my son and hear this lan-
guage."[21]
The fact of the matter was that JRT's middle-aged theatergoers did
not want to accept that picture of their children's generation, with
its self-indulgent, amoral, promiscuous characters. Wollner's
characters are indeed such people, but they are also funny, sensitive,
vivid. Wollner has an infallible ear and the ability to tune in on today's
young Americans, Jewish and otherwise. What Wollner had to say
is sharp, biting and honest.

Wollner grew up in the least Jewish of surroundings. He was raised
in Rye, New York, a wealthy predominantly Christian suburban community, and in Riverdale, New York. "It sort of enhanced my sense
of being Jewish. Although I am not religious, I feel a strong identity," he says.[22] It was reinforced by his family's affiliation with a
reformed Judaism temple, where he attended Sunday School until
he was confirmed at the age of 14. Both cummunities would provide
fertile territory at a later point for Wollner plays, and it is not surprising that his plays would focus on the theme of the outsider.

Wollner enrolled at the University of Wisconsin (the setting for
Badgers) planning to become a lawyer. But he transferred to Adel-
phi University in Garden City, Long Island, where he discovered
theater and in 1970 received his Bachelor of Arts degree in drama.
"I was an actor at first, but a bad actor," he recalls, "before I turned
to playwriting."[23]

The theater was a natural choice. As a child he was talkative, out-
going, a stand-up comic. Moreover, he wrote easily. "It always
seemed to be something I could do a little better than other people—
when I had the right subject."[24]

After graduation he turned to playwriting, studying at the HB Studio with Richard Longchamps and Herbert Berghof for several years.
Wollner recalls,

> I got a very good grounding in playwriting. It was a
> parochial approach, just what I needed, the rudimentary,
> how-to of playwriting, the necessity, for example, to lose
> control in the process, to allow your creativity to take con-
> trol of what you write. I needed to learn that.[25]

Both Wollner and Cohen were members of New Dramatists in the mid-1970s, where they met and "we found we liked each other." Cohen, serving on New Dramatists panels, was "extremely opinionated, right to the point, which was wonderful," Wollner says. "I found his comments useful. And so we formed a relationship."[26]

Once at JRT, Cohen continued to work closely with Wollner, helping him develop both *Badgers* and *Escape from Riverdale*. The latter was barely completed as the show was being cast at the JRT. "There were huge rewrites, and Ed was very involved at that period," Wollner says.[27]

Wollner considers *Badgers* his first real play, despite several earlier efforts.

> It's the first one I still think is O.K. The one I got into
> New Dramatists with, called *Losers*, had some things I
> still like, and there was my first play they produced at
> the Manhattan Punch Line, but I'm not interested in having any one look at these any more.[28]

Wollner feels that early efforts should not be reworked, that one is better off discarding and moving on. But notebooks, he feels, are another matter, often triggering new plays. The second play in *Escape from Riverdale* had just such a genesis.

> I was thumbing through my notebook and I happened on
> a speech about Siddhartha. I thought, "Gee, I like that
> speech. I like that character." It was a play in an old notebook.... But generally old plays should be buried.[29]

Badgers, following its reading at JRT, was produced at the Manhattan Punch Line Theater in 1981 and then published by Samuel French. His plays have also been produced at the Ensemble Studio Theater and in other parts of the country, such as the Beverly Hills Playhouse in Los Angeles and the Unicorn Theater in Kansas City. *Kid Purple* was selected for the 1983 Aspen Playwrights' Conference and was a winner in the Unicorn Theater's National Playwriting Contest. Wollner also received a New York State CAPS grant in 1984.

Despite such professional recognition, Wollner still must earn his living by other means. He has been, in turn, a film script writer, a playreader, an advertising copywriter, an industrial/technical writer. But playwriting "gives me the most pleasure by far." And the best play he has written so far, he feels, is *Kid Purple*. A controversial work with its detractors and its admirers, the play opened to mixed reviews at the Manhattan Punch Line in November 1984. Cohen was not one of the admirers. "Ed didn't want it for JRT," Wollner says. Cohen did not see it as a play with a Jewish theme. While anti-Semitism is the implied theme, Cohen did not feel that the play dealt with the subject pointedly.

Wollner had in fact opted for symbolism. It is the tale of a prizefighter who was born purple from the neck up, a protagonist who fights to turn a stigma into an asset.

> The play is different stylistically from anything else I've written, much less realisitc. It's more pure comedy, like *Hellzapoppin*. I was looking for an active protagonist, but one I could identify with. And I came upon the first Jewish heavyweight, originally called Kid Schwartz. I kept the Jewish characters Jewish. Their name is Schwartz. But I made him purple from the neck up because I needed to give him something to fight against. At that point I lost Ed Cohen, but I won the war, because I had a much better play, and a play which is more accessible to other audiences. It's an absurd, free-form comedy, hopefully with some heart and soul in it. It's a myth, and I needed a malady of mythic proportions as opposed to real proportions.[30]

Whether *Kid Purple* is Jewish or not, Wollner sees himself as a Jewish playwright—but is quick to add that he does not know what that means.

> I think I am subliminally Jewish, and there's nothing I can do about it. For me it's a familiarity with the qualities of self-doubt, an identity with the outsider. I think that might be sort of nibbling at the corners of it. *Kid Purple* explains that feeling.[31]

SUSAN SANDLER

But clearly Jewish in theme and setting is the current play of Susan Sandler, *Crossing Delancey*, which, after a 1984 fall reading, was produced the spring of 1985 at the JRT. The play not only deals with a modern young Jewish-American woman, but also carries clear resonances of an earlier time and place in Jewish history. It is the world of the once vibrant lower East Side, a world which Susan Sandler says still exists in small enclaves below 14th Street.

Nevertheless, like most of her fellow PIRs, Susan Sandler sees herself as not essentially or exclusively a Jewish writer and points out that labels, in any event, are not useful. "It is one thread of many threads that runs through my experience," she says. "In fact, this is the first play that draws on that experience, and it may be the last. The universality is what I'm interested in."[32] This is not to say she denies her heritage. On the contrary. But the Jewish influence is only part of a background which has been tempered by strikingly different college experiences, by northern and southern living.

Born in New York, Sandler was raised in Newport News, Virginia. "I want to write a play about that some time—growing up Jewish in a non-Jewish southern community."[33] But summers were spent visiting her grandmother on New York's lower East Side, a milieu that would provide the raw material for *Crossing Delancey*.

A successful actress as well as playwright, she has always pursued both careers in tandem, and both were evidenced at an early age. "My interest in theater began when I was eight, acting in community theater in Newport News," she recalls, "and I started writing in junior high school."[34] In high school Sandler won a poetry award from the Virginia Poets Society, an award presented to her by Archibald MacLeish. (One of the poems, "Ode to the Pickle Lady," was based on her New York visits and would surface later in *Crossing Delancey*.)

Sandler went on to college in the north, majoring in theater and acting at Boston University's "strong theater department." But illness forced her return to Virginia, where she finished college at Virginia Commonwealth University in Richmond. It was, as she views it, a fortuitous change. The smaller drama department gave Sandler wider opportunities to perform, direct, and write.

Upon graduation, she went immediately to a "wonderful theater in Sarasota, Florida, called the Asolo, the only truly rotating rep in the country, where I got my Equity card."[35] Within two years, pursuing the mainstream of the theater world, Sandler had moved to New York, where she proceeded to work at a number of off-Broadway and off-off-Broadway theaters—CSC Rep, Manhattan Theater Club, Cafe LaMama and Soho Rep among them. She also scripted and produced a docudrama called *Women Against Rape*, which was aired through the Public Broadcasting System in the 1978-79 season.

Sandler began her association with JRT as an actress when she appeared in the role of Lulu in Pinter's *Birthday Party* in January 1981. "At the time I was also writing a play called *Companion Pieces* and Tony McKay (director of *Birthday Party*) brought it to Ed Cohen's attention and we had a fine reading of it there."[36]

In addition to *Companion Pieces*, her plays have included: *The Moaner, The Renovation* and *Three Wilgus Stories*, all of which have been presented at the Ensemble Studio Theater, where she is a member. *The Renovation* was also staged at the Actors Theater of Louisville, a theater which has commissioned her to write another piece. Her plays have also had productions and/or readings at Playwrights Horizons, the West Bank Theater and the Image Theater.

The theme of family relationships as they exist in the 1980s dominates Sandler's work.

> I am interested, as a woman, in the experience of my generation in finding and making families. I seem to go back to that all the time—family bonding of all descriptions: weekend memories, live-in lovers, working mothers with young children, single mothers and fathers—the whole crazy salad of today's familes.[37]

Renovation explores the relationship between a New York teenage girl (child of divorced parents) and her father's lover, a woman who functions as a surrogate mother during the child's weekend visits. "It explores that whole gray area of women who become involved with the children of their lovers," Sandler says.[38] The play, which Sandler sees as probably her favorite, "a strong piece," was staged in Louisville in the 1983-84 season and will, she hopes, go on to a New York production.

Crossing Delancey also examines a family relationship—in this case, the bond between a granddaughter and her grandmother (her *Bubbie*, to cite the Yiddish term used in the play). It is clearly autobiographical and represents Sandler's need to connect with the voice of her own grandmother. "That voice has been a vivid presence in my life."[39] *Crossing Delancey* depicts a young woman's struggle to choose between conflicting values and cultures. The *Bubbie* of Sandler's play and of memory is a notable character, sharply but lovingly defined.

Ran Avni disliked the character, though he had faith enough in the play itself, upon hearing it read, to plan for a full production.

> I was surprised by his reactions. He referred to Bubbie
> at one point as ''the old bitch.'' I never heard that
> response from anybody but him. Every one else loved
> that character. She is funny, tough, loving and strong,
> as women of that generation were. I found his reaction
> surprising, and, I think, off the mark.[40]

Nonetheless, follow-up discussions with Avni and Cohen were fruitful, as were audience responses to the reading. Out of both came the necessary rewrites.

> What I learned from the reading was the way the play
> flowed, how the audience reacted, what moved well,
> where the connective tissue was working and where it
> wasn't. That is something you feel on an intuitive basis
> as you are listening to the play being read.[41]

Playwriting has come to be the dominant force in Sandler's professional life. She continues to act, if an interesting role comes her way, but she no longer auditions. ''When things are offered and the time feels right, I can invest myself in that,'' she says, ''but it is not my real passion. The writing is.''[42]

MICHAEL TAAV

For Michael Taav as well, playwriting has yet to provide an income. Most of his income has been derived through screenwriting, through grants and through teaching assignments, such as the College of New Rochelle and Medger Evers College, which is part of the City University of New York system.

His plays are not as accessible as that of his peers, which may explain why they have taken longer to reach better-known New York stages and to be accepted by audiences. His plays have been produced at colleges on the west coast and at the Gallery Theater in North Carolina; his New York experience, however, has been confined mainly to readings. But Cohen sees him as a playwright with ''a brilliant ear and a unique vision—and is likely one of these days to hit it.''[43] Cohen adds, ''he is the most difficult for us to do, because it is such strange work. Productions here would not do him any good.''[44]

The Taav plays deal with ''moral issues of one sort or another,'' a familiar PIR theme, but handled differently. Sam Shepard has had a strong influence on his work and writing techniques, which has proved a stumbling block for Ed Cohen.

> We used to have these wonderful meetings, and I would talk about how to restructure the play, and he would listen, but he would come back with a new play instead of a rewrite. Sam Shepard never rewrites, so the legend goes. His entire work is one long rewrite. And Michael too.[45]

Finally Cohen told Taav that he could not work that way. "I need a play that is disciplined and structured, so why don't you find another director. He asked me, 'Is this the kiss-off?' and I told him it was."[46]

Realizing that Ed Cohen was serious, Taav at last returned with a rewrite of the play *Home Bodies*, a play that would eventually be produced at St. Marks. A rewrite of *Hard Knocks* followed and the play was given a staged reading at the JRT in 1982-1983. *Hard Knocks* deals with four marginal characters, three of whom survive through petty crimes, and their struggle for power. Taav manages, with minimal language and a stripped-down plot and set, to convey an explosive situation and powerful emotions. Taav says it is "a romance, but not a prototypical romance."[47] The influence of Beckett, Mamet and Shepard are evident, but the voice is original.

Producer Lynn Holtz, on staff at the Public Theatre, had taken an option on *Hard Knocks*, along with Taav's companion piece *Philosopher King*. Both have had a staged reading at the Public in December 1984. Taav sees it as the first step that will, he hopes, lead to a full production. *Hard Knocks*, though read at the JRT, is not a Jewish play in any sense, but rather a play about the twentieth century. Taav says that he is not conspicuously a Jewish playwright, although many of his characters are Jewish, but the Jewishness surfaces in his language.

> Syntactically my work strikes me as being quite Jewish, especially in monologues where the characters ask themselves rhetorical questions, which I see my relatives doing. It's an element of self-propulsion.[48]

Taav, like others, sees his Jewishness as only part of the experience that feeds his work. "One is in a large measure a product of one's environment, and I come from a Jewish environment, but it's not the only environment I've been in."[49]

Taav was born and raised in Brooklyn and, like Donald Margulies, attended SUNY at Purchase, where he, too, came under the influence of Julius Novick. He graduated in 1974 with a degree in literature. Earlier, he had written poetry and short stories, but turned completely to playwriting in college. He went on to graduate school at the University of California at Davis, where a number of his plays were produced. Returning to New York Taav began to ''walk my scripts around and one of the places I walked into was Playwrights Horizons, where Ed was reading.''[50] Cohen particularly liked *Home Bodies*. ''There was something wonderful there.''[51] The play had a reading at Playwrights Horizons, and the Cohen/Taav relationship began. Though no Taav plays have been produced at JRT, there have been two readings, which Taav says he has found helpful.

DAN ELLENTUCK

PIR Dan Ellentuck has had even less contact than the other playwrights with JRT since the PIR program was formed, though Cohen insists that the lines of communication are always open. Since JRT's reading of Ellentuck's *Fat Fell Down* in 1979-80, the playwright has written nothing that Cohen likes. The earlier play, Cohen says, ''was a gem of an idea that had so many wonderful things in it, but he never did figure it out enough to finish it.''[52] The play, both funny and poignant, deals with the adventures of a 13-year-old sent to a camp for overweight boys. ''It was given an excellent staged reading, and it wasn't easy to do or cast, with a cast of 11,'' says Ellentuck. ''And Ed gave me good suggestions, but I never quite worked out all its problems.''[53]

Ellentuck moved on to other works.

> A specific Jewish social situation was involved in *Fat Fell Down*, and I haven't written that way since. I don't think it's possible to banish what you are from your writing, and I don't, but I think the element of ''this is a play clearly of interest to Jews and about Jews'' hasn't been in my stuff since.[54]

He has since had a production at the Capital Repertory Company in Albany of his play *Alice and Fred*, a play that ''Ed had a particular revulsion to,'' which has been optioned for off-Broadway. He has also collaborated on a musical called *Svelte Anna*. The title is a play on words on the name Svetlana, Stalin's daughter, and is based on her life. Currently he is formulating a play about a 1960s commune—"A group of radicals holed up in the Ohio countryside."[55] The dominant theme in his work is the familiar one of "the outsider trying to come to terms with his alienation."[56]

And, like other PIRs, he comes from a decidedly Jewish background. He was born and raised in New York City in an Orthodox Jewish home. He was sent to a Jewish day school through fourth grade, an English-speaking school that offered some instruction in Hebrew. After New York public schools, he attended Antioch College in Ohio and graduate school at Florida State University, majoring in playwriting. "I was stage-struck as a teen-ager and originally wanted to be an actor, but at age 20 realized that playwriting was the stronger field for me," he says.[57]

After graduation he headed for New York, armed with *Fat Fell Down* and several other plays-in-process. He met Cohen when his friend Bo Walker was stage manager for John Galsworthy's *Loyalties* at the JRT in March 1979. "Bo thought Ed might be interested in *Fat Fell Down* and brought it to his attention."[58] Though his contact with JRT has been minimal, to date, he would like more involvement "though I'm afraid that the kind of things I'm writing now are not appropriate for their production needs."[59]

Like other playwrights, Ellentuck continues to earn his living by other means—in his case, as a word processor operator. He writes at night and in the early morning and continues to show work to directors and friends in the business. Does he see himself primarily as a playwright? "I suppose it wouldn't be fair to say I'm a playwright when I spend so much time typing for other people, but I aspire to be a playwright," he summarizes.[60]

RICHARD SCHOTTER

Richard Schotter, on the other hand, though he has stature in two—in fact, several—professions, has no problems with identity. He sees himself clearly as a playwright. "I was hired on the basis of being a playwright, not an academician, to teach at Queens College," he explains.[61] He is a professor in the English Department, teaching courses in dramatic literature as well as playwriting. With a Ph.D. in dramatic literature from Columbia University, he had been a Fulbright Scholar and has compiled, edited and written the introduction to the anthology, *The American Place Theater: Plays*, published by Delta in 1973. Moreover, he has also been a theater critic, an editor of *The Drama Review*, and, from 1971 to 1973, Literary Manager of The American Place Theater.

His interest in show business goes back to early years. Born and raised in the Bronx, he was, as a youngster, part of a rock and roll band. He had plans to become a star and go on tour, an idea that his parents vetoed. Later his interests were channeled into writing, as he went through the New York public schools, New York University and Columbia University.

In recent years his plays have gained recognition and awards. His first play, *Medicine Show: An American Entertainment*, was produced at the Theater of St. Clement's in 1972-1973, toured the United States, Canada and Europe and, in 1973, was nominated for an Obie Award. His second play, *Benya the King*, brought him a New York State CAPS grant in playwriting and also won the 1983 Berman Playwriting Award for the best play on a Jewish theme, sponsored by the National Foundation for Jewish Culture.

Benya has had a substantial history, which began with a reading at the JRT in 1978-1979 and a full production in December 1979. The play also had a production at the Cleveland Jewish Community Center Theater in 1982. The play was inspired by two stories from *Tales of Odessa* by the Russian-Jewish writer Isaac Babel. It deals with a little-known aspect of Jewish life in Russia, with the assimilated, worldly Jews of Odessa, Russia's southern metropolis. Benya is a kind of Robin Hood, who robs from the rich and gives to the poor. Moreover, he is a smooth-talking rogue who builds an empire of crime. Schotter traces his rise and fall and rise again. "It had originally been writtern as a musical, but I decided to forget the musical idea and redid it as a straight play," Schotter says.[62] Schotter sent the unsolicited manuscript to the JRT in the fall of 1978, and Cohen, upon reading it, called the playwright at once. "Richard had a wonderful sense of language and real craftsmanship," Cohen says.[63]

Cohen scheduled the play for a 1979 spring reading, and director Roger Hendricks Simon, who had been away on assignment, met with Schotter just three weeks before the reading. Both agreed that many basic changes were called for, such as giving the play a more fable-like quality and enlarging the role of the Narrator. It woud be useless to stage the reading without the changes, and more time was needed. But Cohen explained that rescheduling was not possible. "It's now or never," he said. In a whirlwind of activity Schotter rewrote the entire play. "It was the best three weeks of my life in terms of having a job to do in a certain period of time and doing it," so Schotter says. "And the play improved enormously as a result."[64]

Following the reading, one more revision was completed by June, and the play went on to full production in December 1979. Schotter recalls,

> It could have been better, but given the strictures of the time and the limitations of an Equity showcase contract, it was an extraordinarily good production, and allowed us a lot of freedom. Whatever Simon wanted he got—within the limits of the budget—without any artistic constraints from Ed or Ran or from any one.[65]

In the fall of 1983 Cohen asked Schotter to join the PIR program, which brought the group to a total of six. Schotter then brought his next play, *The Wood Dancer*, a play about a Hungarian immigrant in America, to Cohen, who disliked it. "You're wasting your time on it," he told Schotter. Nonetheless, he gave Schotter the staged reading he asked for. It was Cohen's commitment to his writers. (*The Wood Dancer* was subsequently produced in July 1987 by the American Theatre of Actors.)

Schotter sees himself "as a writer who is Jewish," one who writes from a Jewish sensibility. His play, *Taking Stock*, for example, is about two men who run a sporting goods store.

> There's no mention of anything Jewish and yet, from my point of view, they seem unmistakably Jewish—in a certain way, the way they bicker. Philip Roth said somewhere that two powerful influences on his work were Henry James and Henny Youngman. That is pretty much the see-saw on which I seem to teeter—the world of literature and the world of living room bickering. In that sense I see my work as Jewish.[66]

NAHMA SANDROW

Most overtly, consciously Jewish of all the PIRs is Nahma Sandrow. Sandrow joined the group in September 1984, following the success of the show *Kuni-Leml*, for which she wrote the book.

Sandrow, daughter of a rabbi, is a practicing Conservative Jew. "I think probably I am the only person connected with the JRT in any capacity who ever goes to synagogue and keeps kosher," she says.[67] Jewishness, as she understands it, calls for active, positive participation—for observance of holidays, for adherence to the traditions, for serious study of the past. On that basis, she sees neither her fellow PIRs, nor Edward Cohen nor Ran Avni nor the JRT itself, as Jewish. "It's bizarre," she says. "Not only don't they practice Judaism, but they are aggressively ignorant, more ignorant about Jewishness than I am about Zen. Jewishness doesn't enrich their lives, as far as I can see."[68]

She indicates that the JRT has other things to offer, that, for example, it serves as a mutual support system. "It's a cozy place, perhaps because, for one reason, people feel among their own kind, largely. Ed feels that some actors who are Jewish feel liberated working there because it's Jewish, and that is definitely something."[69]

Is the Jewish Repertory Theatre then a misnomer? Yes. Is the theater Jewish? No, says Sandrow. Its works are not based on serious scholarship, on digging carefully into the past. Its practitioners are not seeped in Jewish lore. Cohen disagrees with this view and insists that indeed the historic past is carefully researched when it applies to a particular production. But her relationship with JRT, Sandrow says, has been good. "It's a good place to put on plays—and they gave me money, not much, buy some, which is very rare."[70]

Sandrow, like Schotter, is an academician as well as theater person—and, in her case, more scholar than playwright. She is a full professor at the Bronx Community College, where she teaches remedial writing. She rejects the term "academician," because it is not relevant to the courses she teaches. But, beyond the teaching, "I see myself as a writer, a historian, and I would like to write more books."[71] "I'm interested in theater as cultural history, as part of the community, why the community makes the theater it does," she says.[72]

Both theater and scholarship have been intertwined all her adult life. Born in New York and raised in the suburban community of Woodmere, Long Island, she went to Bryn Mawr College and then

Yale School of Drama, where, in 1970, she received a DFA in theater, literature and history. She entered as a playwriting student but changed her major because "I couldn't write plays by making things up from scratch."[73] Her doctoral thesis on French surrealist theater, entitled *Surrealism: Theater Arts and Ideas*, was later published as a book.

Writing a first book was a heady, compelling experience that spurred her on to write *Vagabond Stars*, a history of Yiddish theater, which was published by Harper & Row in 1977. The project took over three years and called upon her skills as a translator and researcher, since much of the resource material was in Yiddish.

The book led to a show called *Vagabond Stars*, based on Yiddish theater material, which she wrote at the instigation of director-producer Alan Albert. The all-English show, a collection of songs, dances and skits, was produced at the Berkshire Theater Festival in Lenox, Massachusetts, where Albert was director for the theater.

Sandrow says that the show had its failings, and that that summer production seemed to be the end of it, until she met Cohen. The two were on a panel at a conference on Jewish theater, held at Marymount College, New York City, in 1981. Cohen suggested that she rework *Vagabond Stars* as a possibility for JRT. There followed a period of close work with both Cohen and Avni, while the show underwent major revisions. *Vagabond Stars* opened in June 1982 and enjoyed such success with JRT audiences and critics that its run was extended through July.

Sandrow's later theatrical success was *Kuni-Leml*, which ran through the summer of 1983 and enjoyed the same acclaim given *Vagabond Stars*. *Kuni-Leml*, based upon an 1880 musical by Goldfadn, the so-called father of Yiddish theater, is a farce that turns on mistaken identity. *Kuni-Leml* ran through the summer at JRT and, in the fall, was optioned for an uptown production at the Audrey Wood Theater, with the same cast.

For Sandrow, now in her forties and with two small children, the night-time writing sessions have become more difficult, as she juggles home, family, teaching, writing.

> I write after everybody is asleep. I used to be able to do
> that better. I could sit down at the typewriter at 9:30 and
> work. But I find, partly because the children are getting

older and perhaps because I'm getting older, it's really grim.[74]

The whole schedule would fall apart, she says, but for her husband, playwright-businessman William Myers, who assumes a great deal of the family responsibility. "Otherwise, it would all be impossible."[75]

CONCLUSION

In all, the playwrights' program has remained, in its first two years, an informal group held together by Edward Cohen's persona. It has been, in fact, not a group at all, except in Cohen's mind, but, rather, seven PIRs, each of whom has a strong relationship with Cohen.

While the writers have occasionally attended each other's productions and readings, no pre-arranged get-togethers have occurred. All were present at the opening of Margulies's play *Gifted Children* in December 1983 and, after the show, gathered at a nearby cafe for beer and shop talk.

"It was wonderful," Cohen said with his usual enthusiasm for the group. "Just the friendship and the affection they had for each other, and the sense of talking to other writers."[76] Cohen vowed on the spot to schedule more such sessions, but has yet to act on the resolution.

Yet Cohen feels that, over the two years, the program has been an enormous success. "They are all thriving," he says with pride, pointing to the large number of readings and productions his PIRs have had at other theaters. He feels that the JRT encouragement given them at critical times in their careers has furthered that development. Also, he feels that they are more in touch with their Jewish identity as a result of the JRT relationship. Furthermore, he says, it is an association the PIRs are happy to acknowledge. "The identification hasn't hurt them, and whenever they have a show somewhere else, they're sure to list their JRT affiliation in their bios."[77]

How do the playwrights themselves, looking back over two years, evaluate the experience—the program, JRT, their relations with Cohen, their relations with each other? Are they as euphoric as Cohen?

First, they tend to see the "playwright-in-residence" label as titular rather than active. "We haven't yet achieved an identity as a group," says Margulies, "and we haven't become the kind of intellectual enclave I think Ed had envisaged.''[78] Don Wollner agrees.

> We don't meet often enough to have a strong identity with the JRT. And there's no give-and-take among us. I was disappointed, for instance, that none of them commented on my play. I'd love to have had them tell me if they hated it. As professionals, they'd be doing me a favor. Michael Taav came to the play and sent me a lovely note, but none of the others saw it, as far as I know.[79]

Yet both Schotter and Margulies feel that they do have a sense of community at the JRT. ''It's nice to feel you are at home somewhere,'' Margulies says.[80]

There is no disagreement about Edward Cohen. The playwrights are unanimous in their appreciation of the part he has played in their professional growth. They feel great affection for him. And they laud his honesty and good taste and supportiveness. Margulies says,

> He has great generosity of spirit when it comes to young writers. He's been a real friend to me. He wrote a wonderful recommendation for me for the NEA grant. That's an indication of the kind of selfless supporter he is capable of being.[81]

Schotter says,

> Ed gave a reading to my *Wood Dancer* even when he hated it. In most theaters, if somebody hates a play, that's it. But Ed is different. He is committed to you as a writer, and that's a rare thing. There's very little continuity to a writer's life. That's why the JRT, and particularly Cohen, has been so valuable to me.[82]

And Wollner adds, ''Ran and Ed are first-class all the way, and their attitude toward new plays is above reproach.''[83]

The playwrights, while acknowledging Avni's help, view him differently. They see him as more conservative in tastes, more commercial in his views, and more concerned with overall JRT needs as opposed to playwright's needs. Yet Avni, too, has been valuable ''in his open, honest Israeli way,'' as one PIR put it. ''Ran is John Q. Public,'' says Wollner, ''but his comments can be very astute.''[84] Yet all the PIRs would like to see changes, both in the playwrights' program and in the JRT itself. Several of the group would welcome regular playwrights' meetings. Schotter, who does not have a playwrights' group which meets regularly to share and comment on each others' work, would value such an activity. Ellentuck, too, would welcome more involvement, although he says, "I feel funny about making suggestion since my contributions have been so slight."[85]

But most of the PIRs already have such resources. Both Susan Sandler and Don Wollner are members of the playwrights' group at the Ensemble Studio Theater, Donald Margulies has the Writers' Bloc, and Susan Sandler is also a member of the Deborah Project, a women's playwright group at the American Jewish Theatre. And Michael Taav and Dan Ellentuck both have informal groups. Yet all agree that more contact with each other, if the time and logistics could be managed, would be useful. In viewing the JRT itself, the playwrights see it as basically a fine theater that turns out well-crafted works and with a steadily-growing reputation. Michael Taav says,

> It seems to be making a dent. Its works are beginning to move, and all sorts of people are associating themselves with it—Arthur Miller, for instance—and all sorts of performers are quite willing to work there. Its success denotes that it is speaking effectively to its audiences.[86]

There are changes that the playwrights would like to see at the JRT itself. Don Wollner, whose *Escape from Riverdale* suffered at the hands of the JRT audiences, would like to see the theater change its locale and also make a real effort to appeal to younger audiences and to try new material. As Wollner views it,

> I think Ran has to have a steady diet of taking chances, of taking on Jewish writers who write on any theme. The theater has to reflect the entire community, including the younger Jewish community. The question is whether the JRT wants to be a museum or a thriving theater breaking new ground.[87]

Susan Sandler agrees:

> I'd like to see the playwrights responsible for bringing in a lot of new blood in the audiences, taking chances with the kinds of material that might be tough for the regulars.[88]

Both Avni and Cohen insist that they are aware of the problems of limiting programs to a certain kind of audience and are in fact working hard to draw in younger, more adventurous audiences as well. In fact, the whole PIR program is part of the effort to expand horizons.

Donald Margulies sees part of the problem at JRT as due to a limited budget. "There are limitations in lighting, sets, actors, space, advertising—every aspect of production."[89] But, he admits, it is a problem not limited to JRT, and is probably an inevitable part of the whole process. Richard Schotter thinks it would be good to get audience feedback at the readings, a policy not generally followed at the JRT. "Not fancy statements," says Schotter, "but just comments on whether this or that works."[90] Nahma Sandrow, who criticizes the JRT for not being a Jewish theater and sees Jewishness in terms different from her fellow PIRs, says, "What I'm waiting for is somebody to write a gorgeous play in which the allusions and metaphors are going to be Jewish, Jewish-American, with some reference to history that signifies something—and it's going to be terrific."[91]

While the playwrights appreciate their connection, they nevertheless do not feel an exclusive loyalty to the theater. If the Public Theater, for example, were to make a better offer for a production, it would be hard to turn it down. Schotter, who feels the conflict between loyalty and professional opportunity, says, "There is some fear of being pigeon-holed as somebody who just writes Jewish material. It could be limiting."[92] But Susan Sandler is clear on the subject.

> What matters most is the work and where you are going
> to develop the most and where your work is going to be
> treated most carefully. Your commitment, foremost, is
> to your work.[93]

Yet, whatever criticisms and suggestions for change the PIRs might make, they are more than aware of what they have gained from the JRT and the playwrights' program. They have been helped to mature artistically and to gain recognition in the theater world. And that recognition, in turn, has been shared with the JRT. It is all that Ed Cohen had hoped to achieve.

[1]Edward M. Cohen, interview, New York City, 6 December 1984.

[2]Ibid.

[3]Ibid.

[4]Ibid.

[5]Susan Sandler, interview, New York City, 19 November 1984.

[6]Cohen, interview, 6 December 1984.

[7]Ibid.

[8]Don Wollner, interview, 19 October 1984.

[9]Cohen, interview, 6 December 1984.

[10]In addition to the playwrights, Cohen has been adding composers to the group, among them Raphael Crystal, whose work is discussed in Chapter 4.

[11]Donald Margulies, interview, New Haven, Connecticut, 5 October 1984.

[12]Ibid.

[13]Ibid.

[14]Cohen, interview, 6 December 1984.

[15]Margulies, interview, 5 October 1984.

[16]Ibid.

[17]Ibid.

[18]Ibid.

[19]Ibid.

[20]Ibid.

[21]Wollner, interview, 19 October 1984.

[22]Ibid.

[23]Ibid.

[24]Ibid.

[25]Ibid.

[26]Ibid.

[27]Ibid.

[28]Ibid.

[29]Ibid.

[30]Ibid.

[31]Ibid.

[32]Susan Sandler, interview, New York City, 19 November 1984.

[33]Ibid.

[34]Ibid.

[35]Ibid.

[36]Ibid.

[37]Ibid.

[38]Ibid.

[39]Ibid.

[40]Ibid.

[41]Ibid.

[42]Ibid.

[43]Cohen, interview, 6 December 1984.

[44]Ibid.

[45]Ibid.

[46]Ibid.

[47]Michael Taav, interview, New York City, 6 November 1984.

[48]Ibid.

[49]Ibid.
[50]Ibid.
[51]Cohen, interview, 6 December 1984.
[52]Ibid.
[53]Dan Ellentuck, interview, New York City, 16 November 1984.
[54]Ibid.
[55]Ibid.
[56]Ibid.
[57]Ibid.
[58]Ibid.
[59]Ibid.
[60]Ibid.
[61]Richard Schotter, interview, 8 November 1984.
[62]Ibid.
[63]Cohen, interview, 6 December 1984.
[64]Schotter, interview, 8 November 984.
[65]Ibid.
[66]Ibid.
[67]Nahma Sandrow, interview, New York City, 13 November 1984.
[68]Ibid.
[69]Ibid.
[70]Ibid.
[71]Ibid.
[72]Ibid.
[73]Ibid.
[74]Ibid.
[75]Ibid.
[76]Cohen, interview, 6 December 1984.
[77]Ibid.
[78]Margulies, interview, 5 October 1984.
[79]Wollner, interview, 19 October 1984.
[80]Margulies, interview, 5 October 1984.
[81]Ibid.
[82]Schotter, interview, 8 November 1984.
[83]Wollner, interview, 19 October 1984.
[84]Ibid.
[85]Ellentuck, interview, 16 November 1984.
[86]Taav, interview, 6 November 1984.
[87]Wollner, interview, 19 October 1984.
[88]Sandler, interview, 19 October 1984.
[89]Margulies, interview, 5 October 1984.
[90]Schotter, interview, 8 November 984.
[91]Sandrow, interview, 13 November 1984.
[92]Schotter, interview, 8 November 1984.
[93]Sandler, interview, 19 November 1984.

6

The JRT Audience

Theater, the most communal of the arts, involves many participants—playwrights, actors, directors, producers, set designers, stage managers, and so on. But, as we know, the work of art is not complete, does not come alive, until the addition of one final group—the audience. The audience is an indispensable element in the entire process. Audiences must be considered particularly in a study of the Jewish Repertory Theatre. They are in fact unlike audiences anywhere else in this country today. They most closely resemble—in fact are the modern-day counterpart—of the old Yiddish theater audiences. They laugh and cry aloud, express their approval or disapproval in verbal outbursts, and are not above disrupting the performance by discoursing with the actors or stamping noisily out of the theater.

The long-time subscribers, particularly, have a fierce attachment

to their theater. They treat the JRT as if it were a family member—
or rather their child, taking pride in its accomplishments and offering rebukes when it falls short of their standards. At intermission they
indulge in gusty debate among themselves and are likely to confront
artistic director Avni in the lobby, freely airing their views. Fail-
ing that, they write to Avni, to make sure he knows where they stand.

Not all behave in that fashion. The younger theatergoers, more
identified with mainstream theater, take their model from those audiences, and behave with more restraint. But many JRT theatergoers
are beyond fifty years of age and have strong memories of the Yiddish theater experience. They can recall childhood excursions with
their fathers to Maurice Schwartz performances on Second Avenue.
In their nostalgic attachment to the past, they re-enact the scene, even
to duplicating audience behavior.

Who are the people who make up the JRT audiences? From where
do they come? What are their ages, interests, occupations? Why do
they support the JRT? What do they expect of the theater? What do
they commend and what do they criticize?

A recent survey provides, if not a definitive audience profile, at
least a sense of who the JRT theatergoers are. Many, but not all, were
subscribers. By the end of the 1984-85 season subscriptions had
reached 1500, and, in the same season, total attendance figures for
each production ran from a high of 2819 for *Shlemiel the First* to a
low of 1545 for *City Boy*.

In conjunction with this dissertation, 2500 questionnaires were dis-
tributed to these theatergoers, folded into the programs, during the
spring 1985 run of Susan Sandler's *Crossing Delancey*. There was
over a ten percent return, with 265 questionnaires mailed back or
left at the theater. One must take into account the fact that it was probably the theatergoers most committed to the JRT who bothered to
respond, so the results are skewed in that direction. Also, all 265 respondents did not reply to every category in the questionnaire, which
made for variation in totals of each category. Morever, some answers
were confusing or contradictory, due in part to the respondents and
in part to the design of the questionnaire. (For example, when some
respondents indicated that they were unmarried, they did not explain

whether than meant "never married," "divorced," or "widowed.")

Nevertheless, despite the limitations of the sampling, one does get a strong sense of the audience from the responses. The typical JRT theatergoer, one can reasonably conclude, is in the upper fifties in age, Jewish, married, college-educated, professional (or a retired professionl), living in Manhattan (or Brooklyn or Long Island), and a strong supporter of other theaters and other performing arts, particularly music. More likely to be female than male, she has been a subsciber for the past several years. She subscribed because a friend suggested she do so, because she enjoyed earlier productions or because she thought Jewish theater should be supported. She attends most productions because she paid for them and because she expects to enjoy them, although she is occasionally disappointed.

This profile, however, must be immediately contradicted. Looking closely at the responses, one finds at once considerable diversity, with the exception almost as prevalent as the rule. For example, though the larger number are females, there is a mix, with 144 female respondents, 90 male, and the rest indicating no category at all. There is, however, clearly a preponderance of married people, many of whom indicated that they attended as couples. The breakdown was as follows: married—175, widow—15, widower—1, single-31, divorced—8, separated—1. The repsonses also revealed that a frequent reason for attendance was social, with several couples subscribing and attending throughout the year together, coming in from Long Island or New Jersey as a group.

Most of those who responded were subscribers (203 out of 265). Of that number, 68 were new members [figure 1], having subscribed just that season (1985). As many indicated, the enormous success of *Kuni-Leml* had much to do with their decision. The next largest group were those who had been subscribers for three seasons (35 or 17.2 percent). In all, most respondents were relatively new subscribers—with 151 having joined in the previous four years.

The age of attendees [figure 2], according to the 212 who answered the question, showed considerable spread. Despite the average age of 56 and the median age of 59, the respondents ranged in years from 23 to 89. But there were few in their 20s and 30s, with the figures mounting in the 40s. The largest single age group was the 60s, with 74 (or 34.9 percent) respondents from that age group, with 20 of

FIGURE 1

SUBSCRIBERS

(203 responses)*

Questions: Are you a subscriber? For how long?

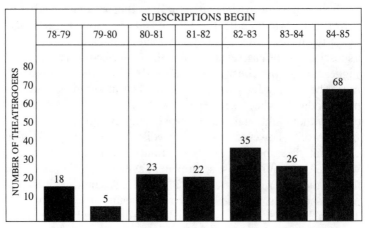

*Although 203 responded, only 197 indicated which year they subscribed.

them indicating that they were exactly 60 years of age.

The theatergoers' educational background [figure 3], on the other hand, is more consistent. One can conclude that the JRT audience is a highly-educated group, in terms of academic credentials. Of the 232 who replied to this question, 88.8 percent held undergraduate college degrees or higher. There were 25 law or medical degrees (10.8 percent of the total) and 17 Ph.D.s (7 percent of the total). The largest single group were those with master's degrees (87 in number or 37.5 percent of the total). Holders of master's and bachelor's degrees, together, made up 70.7 percent of the total. No one had less than a high school diploma, with 19 indicating that they held high school diplomas and seven more stating that they had had some college time.

Religious affiliation was also fairly uniform, with most respondents indicating they were Jewish [figure 4]. However, they differed

FIGURE 2

AGE DISTRIBUTION

(212 responses)

Question: Age?

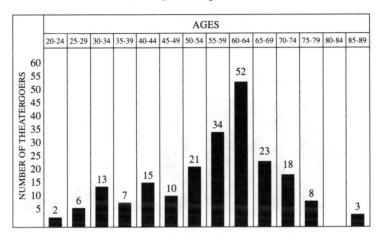

FIGURE 3

EDUCATION

(232 responses)

Question: Education (highest degree)?

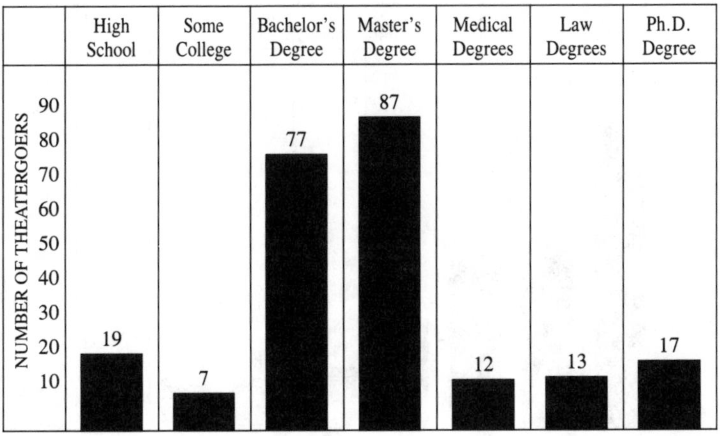

FIGURE 4

RELIGION

(245 responses)

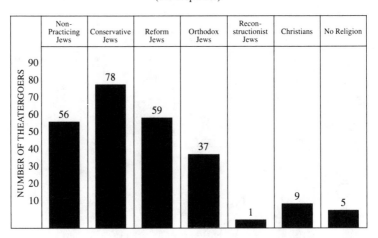

FIGURE 5

ADDRESSES

(156 responses)

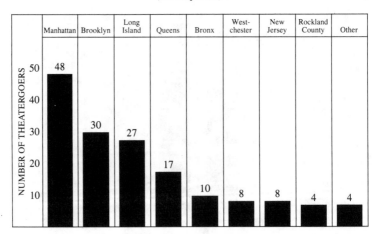

as to religious observance, with practicing Conservative Jews comprising the largest single group. Of the 244 who responded, 13 indicated that they were not Jewish (8 Christian and 5 with no religion). Another 55 indicated that they were non-practicing Jews (i.e., did not belong to a congregation or attend religious services regularly). Those who did consider themselves practicing Jews (175) broke down into four groups: Conservative (78), Reform (59), Orthodox (37), and Reconstructionist (1).

As to place of residence, of the 156 who answered the question, 105 in number, or 67.3 percent, came from New York City [figure 5]. Others, for the most part, were from the outlying areas of Long Island, New Jersey, Westchester and Rockland County. Visitors from more distant locations had come as guests of friends or relatives. Manhattan provided the largest single group, with 47, or 30 percent of the total, with Brooklyn and Long Island following at 30 and 27 replies respectively. Respondents were pretty evenly divided between homeowners and apartment dwellers [figure 6]. Of the 221 who responded to that question, 100, or 45 percent, were homeowners. Apartment renters numbered 79, or 35.7 percent, and those who owned their apartments were 42 in number, or 19 percent. Occupations [figure 7], however, revealed considerable variety, despite the preponderance of professional people (particularly educators) and retirees (many of them former professionals). Retirees made up the largest single group at 48 out of the 222 respondents, and, following closely, were the 47 educators. The two groups together made up 42.8 percent of the total. The total number of professional people was 83 (or 37.4 percent of the total respondents) and included college professors, school administrators, teachers among the educators, as well as scientists, librarians, physicians, dentists, accountants, and attorneys. There were 30 business executives, 14 office workers, 13 in the helping professions (social workers, nurses, counselors), 11 in the fine and performing arts, and 10 who defined themselves as homemakers. At the far end of the scale were a scattering that included a lab technician, city offical, optician, journalist, advertising copywriter, and two students. The general groups listed above, and grouped for convenience, included a much wider diversity than the grouping would indicate, with such occupations listed as actor, art historian, banker, civil engineer, computer analyst,

FIGURE 6

DWELLINGS

(221 respondents)

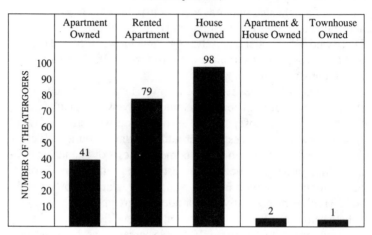

FIGURE 7

OCCUPATIONS

(222 responses)

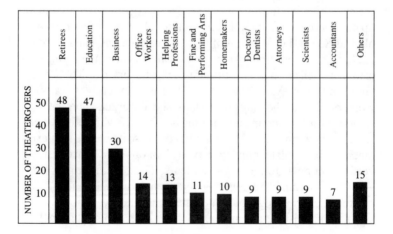

filmmaker, judge, nutritionist, television director, sculptor, textile designer, cab driver/writer. Despite variations in occupations, there is a homogeneity to the group, provided by the large number of professionals and retirees.

Responses to the question of income [figure 8] were most surprising of all, with the answers fluctuating wildly. There appeared to be a reluctance to answer the question, despite the fact that respondents did not have to reveal their names. Only 195 replied to the question, as compared to well over 200 for most other questions. In any event, those who did respond revealed annual incomes ranging from under $15,000 to over $80,000. A good proportion (128 people or 65.6 percent) of the incomes fell between the range of $15,000 to $59,999, with 66 respondents (the largest single group) earning between $35,000 and $59,999. There were, however, seven people who reported annual incomes of less than $15,000, while a sizeable number (39) indicated incomes of $80,000 or more. One explanation for the incomes at the low end of the scale could be the number of retirees, as well as the several students and actors, who responded.

FIGURE 8
ANNUAL INCOMES
(195 responses)

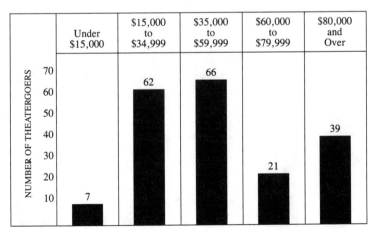

Moving away from the personal data, one finds a wide number of reasons why the JRT supporters chose to subscribe [figure 9]. The question sparked much editorial comment and highly individualized responses. Nevertheless, certain views appeared again and again. Of the 214 responses, 55 indicated they had been impressed with earlier productions (mentioning such shows as *My Heart Is in the East, Awake and Sing!* and particularly *Kuni-Leml*), 31 said they were drawn to Jewish themes, 18 felt they wanted to support Jewish theater, 18 had had the theater recommended to them, 19 felt that the price was right, and 19 joined simply because they liked theater. Geographic location and convenience was the major drawing card for 13, and the JRT's "good reputation" influenced six others. Nine people said it was an experience that could be shared with friends or relatives. Four others indicated that it was a way to be sure they had tickets for all the shows. A few said that they enjoyed off-Broadway theater or were interested in ethnic theater, while several others subscribed on the basis of good press reviews. Still others subscribed

FIGURE 9

WHY THEY SUBSCRIBED

(214 responses)

Question: Why did you subscribe?

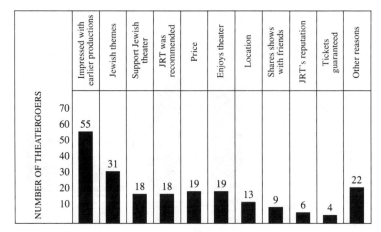

because they found the theater "folksy," "earthy," "innovative," "upretentious," "intimate," and "enjoyable." Other individual responses of note: "I did it on a whim." "My wife subscribed." "I thought it was a way to meet young people." "I knew Ran Avni." And, finally, two people answered the question with another question, typical of those with an Eastern European Yiddish background, "Why not?"

Asked if they, as subscribers, attended all performances [figure 10], of the 207 who responded, 162 said that they attended all and 15 said "most." Thirty said no, giving a variety of reasons as to why they were selective—if they were out of town or ill or if they had heard the show was poor or had depressing subject matter. As to the reasons for attending all productions, 44 people replied, "Because I have a subscription." Not surprisingly, reponses explaining reasons for attending productions were often similar to reasons given for subscribing. Seven replied, "Because I love theater," and 15 said that they enjoyed JRT performances generally. Two indicated that the theater was nearby, and two others said that it provided pleasant Sunday experiences. Individuals also said that the price was right, that they hoped for good entertainment, and that they liked to support Jewish theater. Other responses: "I like a night on my own." "It's theater at its best." "My wife makes me." "I'll try anything," and again, the Talmudic response, "Why not?"

One of the most revealing questions of all, in terms of the audiences' relations to the theater, was: "In what way is the JRT a 'Jewish theater' to you?" [See figure 11.]

Of the 181 who responded to that question, 145 (or 80.1 percent) felt it was indeed a Jewish theater and gave a variety of reasons for thinking so. The majority of that group (117 out of the 145) felt that the theater was definitely Jewish because it featured Jewish playwrights or plays with Jewish themes, characters, setting, thus providing a link to the past and present culture. Ten indicated that the theater was Jewish because the shows were easy to identify with, nine because it was located at the the YMHA, and five because one was "surrounded by fellow Jews." Other explanations: "It offers a Jewish type of humor." "It promotes new talents." "It has a responsive, talkative audience." "It's close to the Lower East Side."

But 36 held a different view, with 17 indicating that the JRT only

FIGURE 10

PERFORMANCE ATTENDANCE

(207 responses)

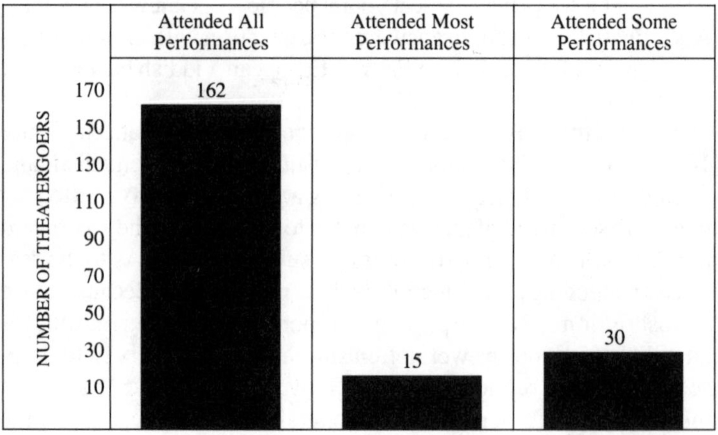

	Attended All Performances	Attended Most Performances	Attended Some Performances
170	162		
150			
130			
110			
90			
70			
50			
30			30
10		15	

NUMBER OF THEATERGOERS

FIGURE 11

JRT AS JEWISH THEATER

(181 responses)

Question: Is the JRT a "Jewish theater" to you?

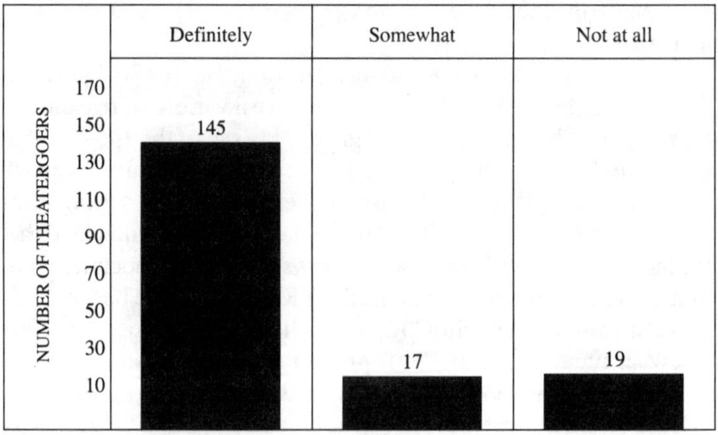

	Definitely	Somewhat	Not at all
170			
150	145		
130			
110			
90			
70			
50			
30			19
10		17	

NUMBER OF THEATERGOERS

occasionally presented Jewish themes and was "somewhat Jewish," and 19 insisting that it was in "no way" Jewish. One respondent, however, softened that comment by adding that the JRT was good off-Broadway theater. Other comments: "It enables me to experience a Jewish world." "It brings Jewish light to my heart." And, last of all, "Is the theater Jewish? Sometimes I wonder."

Looking at the theater and its productions more specifically, the JRT audience named its most favorite and least favorite productions, expressed views on the theater's physical plant and its 14th Street location, and suggested changes it would like to see effected.

As to favorite plays [figure 12], the audience was enthusiastic enough to name, not one, but several all-time favorites. But the musical *Kuni-Leml* outstripped 29 other choices by far, showing a unanimity rare among JRT audiences. It garnered 118 of the 353 total votes, the nearest play to that being *Crossing Delancey* with 58 votes. Some of the comments were, "It made me laugh and cry." "Fresh and imaginative." "Beautifully produced." "Entertaining and Jewish." "Great music." "Heartwarming." As to *Crossing Delancey*,

FIGURE 12

FAVORITE JRT PLAYS

(353 responses)

Question: Your favorite JRT plays?

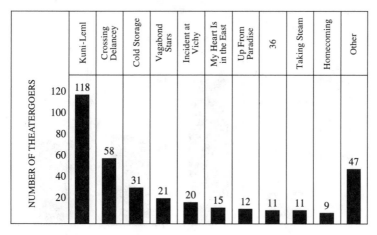

FIGURE 13

LEAST FAVORITE JRT PLAYS

(181 responses)

Question: What productions did you like the least?

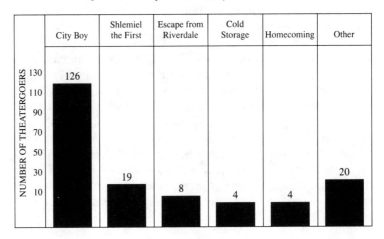

FIGURE 14

THEATER SPACE

(178 responses)

Question: What do you think of the theater space itself?

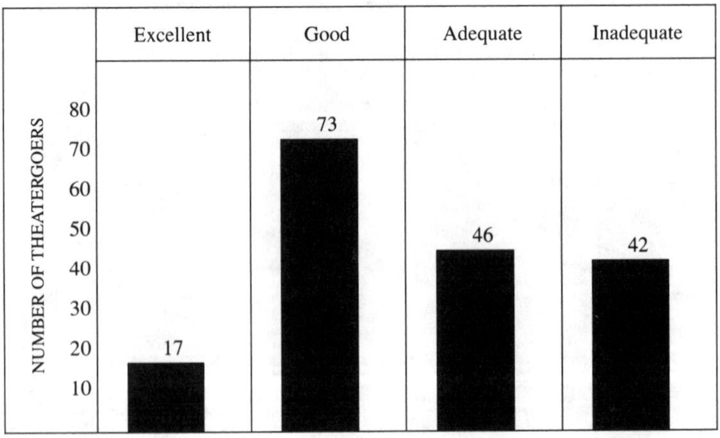

fans commented, "That's what the JRT is all about." And "It's what we expect of the JRT." Others added, "Nostalgic and funny." "Hits home." "Touching." *Cold Storage*, which viewers saw as "thought-provoking but depressing," amassed 31 votes. Other popular choices were *Vagabond Stars* (21 votes), *Incident at Vichy* (20), *My Heart Is in the East* (15), and *Up From Paradise* (12). From there the votes dwindled for the remaining 23 choices, from 11 down to a single vote for each of nine plays. A few respondents replied, "almost all productions" and "anything with Joe Silver."

The audience was equally vehement, vocal and unanimous in its choice of least favorite play—*City Boy*, the contemporary, abrasive Leonard Michaels stories which Edward Cohen had adapted for the stage [figure 13]. The play received 126 of the 181 negative votes. Comments were indeed strong: "doesn't belong in a Y," "we felt used," "gratuitous vulgarity," "offensive," "incomprehensible," "made fun of Jewish values," "didn't work," "boring," "pointless," "gloomy," "wierd," "sleazy," "dumb," "oi!" Isaac Singer's play *Shlemiel the First* took 19 negative votes—"badly written" and "showed worse side of past Jewish life," and *Escape from Riverdale* ("amateurish and "too much vulgarity"") warranted eight. In all, respondents had singled out 17 plays for dislike, some of which, such as Pinter's *The Homecoming* and Arthur Miller's *Incident at Vichy*, had been chosen by others as favorites.

As to the theater space itself, the physical plant, three-fourths of the respondents found it acceptable, while the remaining quarter, highly verbal in its criticsm, did not [figure 14]. Specifically, 50.6 percent of the 178 respondents found it good or excellent, another 25.8 percent said it was adequate, and 23.6 percent saw it as inadequate. The critics pointed out that the space was "too small," "sterile," "cold in winter," "dismal," "not comfortable or atmospheric." Several commented that the ceiling was too low for the back rows, where people bumped their heads when they stood. Another said, "It needs more defined theater space."

Others felt just the opposite, with 31 people insisting that they found the setting "comfortable and intimate." Other positive comments: "nice to see what they do with stage limitation," "ideal for new productions," "feels like family," "lighting and set design is tops," and finally, "good visibility even from the back."

FIGURE 15

THEATER LOCATION

(208 responses)

Question: What do you think of the JRT location at the Midtown Y?

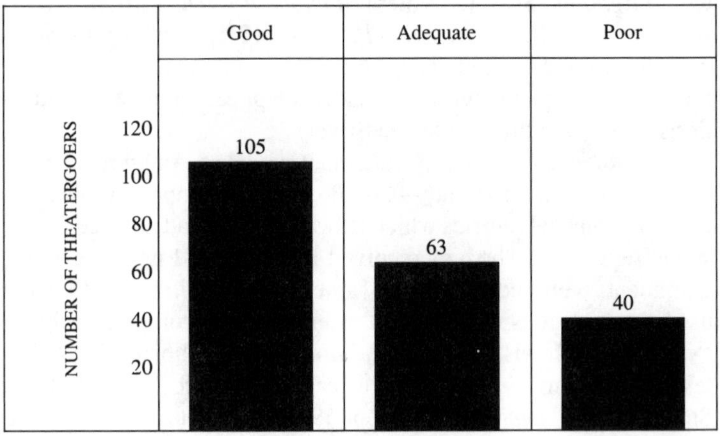

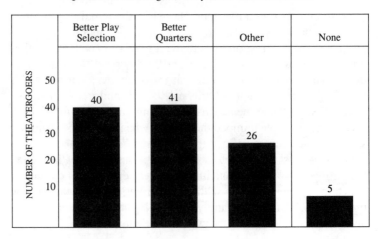

FIGURE 16

DESIRED CHANGES

(112 responses)

Question: What changes would you like to see at the JRT?

The question about the theater's 14th Street location brought 208 responses, with 105 (or about half) finding it good, another 63 (30.3 percent) finding it adequate, and 40 (19.2 percent) insisting it was bad [figure 15]. Those who approved offered such reasons as the convenient parking, nearby restaurants or the fact that they lived in the neighborhood. One respondent also pointed out, "it's appropriate considering the social significance of the Lower East Side to the Jewish people." The critics, however, objected strenuously to 14th Street, describing it as dirty, dangerous and drug-ridden.

Only 112 theatergoers answered the question, "What changes would you like to see at the JRT?" But those 112 had a good deal to say. Only five indicated that they were satisfied with the ways things were, but one can assume that many of those who did not answer the question at all were satisfied. In general, people asked for "a better selection of plays" (40) and "better quarters" (41), not always specifying what they meant by either answer [figure 16]. But some were very specific about the plays, calling for "more serious plays," "plays with a message," "plays with Jewish context," "livelier material," "good revivals," "no more homosexuality," "no more experimental plays," and "no more *City Boys*."

In asking for better quarters, many did not specify what that meant, but others spelled out their requirements clearly: "better location," "more comfortable seats," "air-conditioning," "better lobby," "more emergency exits," "cleaner toilets," "a higher ceiling over the back rows." I would suspect that, in addition to wanting more physical comfort and more pleasant surroundings, they wanted to be able to take more pride in "their" theater.

There were 26 other suggested changes that did not fall into either category. Eight respondents asked for more advance publicity of shows and for synopses in playbills, particularly of new plays. They asked for more matinees, for shows to start on time and for after-show discussions. They called for better actors, directors, productions and for nicer personnel in the Y office to handle their calls. They asked that ticket prices not be escalated. They suggested that refreshments be sold at intermission. One man asked for "for more plays with Joe Silver," and another suggested that the JRT bring travelling shows to senior citizen centers in the New York area. One Orthodox respondent aked that shows be started later on Saturday nights in good weather, since the Jewish sabbath does not end till sundown. Finally, one theatergoer called for "gradual improvement in all phases."

EDITORIAL COMMENTS

Both the personal data and the questions concerning the theater itself, as reviewed above, yielded a good deal of information about the JRT theatergoers. But personal information is revealed not so much through the quantitative material as through their editorial comments, culled both from the questionnaire and from letters received at the JRT office. Ultimately the JRT audiences must be dealt with in narrative rather than statistical fashion, if one is to get a true sense of these theatergoers.

Although many filled out the questionnaires in a perfunctory manner, asnwering the questions they selected conscientiously but briefly, others provided more telling comments, revealing much more of the audience relationship to the JRT.

For instance, one respondent wrote, "I subscribed because I thought I was getting a bargain. Little did I know!" The comment carried the self-mocking, ironic tone so typical of the Yiddish people and language, and probably meant just the opposite—namely, that the subscription was not a bargain at all. But later, during the intermission of *Crossing Delancey*, the writer added a postscript, "I loved all of it; so full of good humor and truth!" Apparently, the JRT was forgiven for past sins and had redeemed itself.

Another theatergoer from the upper west side of Manhattan wrote that the theater was "hard to get to, but worth it if the play is good," and added that she wished the JRT would run "good revivals rather than poor new plays." An 89-year-old woman, who continues to pursue many interests subscribed because she lives in the neighborhood and it is convenient.

Another would like to see "plays that do not make me shudder for their superficiality, like *Delancey Street* [*Crossing Delancey*]," and suggested "plays with cranial muscle like Ibsen." A Long Island woman, on the other hand, writes that she was born on the Lower East Side, so *Crossing Delancey* was particularly meaningful.

Another viewer (who happened to be a stage technician who had worked on some JRT shows) suggested that "the lighting booth should be cleaned up and sound-proofed, so that you don't hear the technicians talking.''

A woman from Queens wrote that she found something good in every JRT show. ''Each is unique and pleasurable on its own.'' A Westchester woman wondered how they make money in such a small theater, but a retired businessman pointed out that the theater does wonders with a limited budget. ''The excellent acting and casting and direction are your strength!''

Viewers, who said they could not afford Broadway prices, appreciated the ticket prices, and a physician agreed, saying, ''It's cheap, folksy, earthy.'' A Bronx woman added that the theater is ''not the greatest, but any move would increase expenses, so stay where you are!''

But a Manhattan salesman focussed on other than expenses, complaining that the seating arrangement for subscribers was unfair. ''In all the time I've been coming to the JRT I have never sat center theater at any level!''

Viewers said they would like to see more translations of Yiddish and Hebrew plays and such plays as *The Dybbuk, The Golem,* and *God of Vengeance*, while one respondent called for ''a penetrating illumination of middle-class American life,'' and another for plays, not necessarily Jewish, but ''innovative and creative.''

One of the few non-Jewish subscribers said that she did not in any way view the JRT as Jewish, but that it was good, humane theater.

A Queens engineer called for more advance information about plays, particularly when the theme was obscure. ''It's difficult to ask people to join you, when all you know is the name.'' One Brooklyn couple subscribed, they said, because such theater should be kept ''alive and available.'' One Long Island couple, four-year subscribers, were highly enthusiastic. ''We love your productions— good acting, good plays and a Jewish experience. We try never to miss any!'' And a newcomer said she would certainly come back for future performances. ''The JRT reinforces my feeling about my Jewish identity,'' said a retired schoolteacher. ''I for one like the idea of the theater being connected with the Y,'' said one 65-year-old woman. ''I feel more at home, like I'm touching base in such an environment.''

''Where are the good writers?'' a Brooklyn subscriber asked. ''I really haven't the time or patience to sit through a new play that's junk...." But other Brooklyn subscribers countered, "In six or seven years, there were only three or four bad productions. So who's complaining?"

A Queens teacher wrote, "I especially like JRT when my mother or other out-of-town guests visit. Every one I've ever taken to JRT has enjoyed that more than the Broadway plays they've seen."

LETTERS TO THE JRT

More impassioned than the questionnaire responses were letters received at the JRT office over the years.[1] If people took the trouble to write Avni letters, it was because they cared—one way or the other—to let him know what they thought. Generally, they made the effort more often when they disliked the play.

One woman, for instance, felt strongly enough about Don Wollner's *Escape from Riverdale*, staged in April 1984, to write a lengthy letter, which said in substance:

> Since when is rape a topic for comedy? We have also
> heard four-letter words and we know their meaning, but
> their constant repetition belied the paucity of the author's
> talents....I have no quarrel with struggling young authors
> who wish to experiment with new ideas...but to present
> it to an audience such as the one you know is watching
> and to whom you appeal for contributions...is an insult.

Avni felt impelled to defend the theater in a reply written a week later:

> We...are firmly committed to do works that reflect the
> Jewish experience as a whole, not just those appealing
> to middle-class audiences that seek some sort of Jewish
> identification in the modern theater....The artists who
> work here...represent all classes, ages, interests and
> tastes.[2]

While most of the *Riverdale* letters were written in a similar vein ("an unredeeming ordeal to inflict upon an audience"), one letter took a different tack: "When we saw the play we laughed without stopping. We recommended it to friends who liked it very much but thought it was very sad."

City Boy brought in an avalanche of critical mail. One New Jersey letter summed up the prevailing attitude: "Regardless of what selection process you used...it was as if you'd had a lobotomy, gotten high on cocaine and other drugs....I left after 30 minutes of utter profanity and garbage conversation.''

Kuni-Leml was the exception to the rule that people wrote to complain rather than praise. The JRT was engulfed with laudatory notes after the show opened in June 1984: ''immensely enjoyed it,'' ''saw the show three times,'' ''took a former Benedictine monk and his wife, a former nun—and couldn't think of a better show to take them to. They loved it.''

But between the extremes of *Kuni-Leml* and *City Boy* lay most JRT productions, plays that some audiences liked and others did not. Responses to *Anna Kleiber*, staged in March 1978, typified much of the audience mail. ''Just to tell you my friend and I enjoyed the performance....excellent job...a fascinating play and the staging and every line in it did it justice...keep up the good work,'' wrote one woman. But an outraged subscriber wrote, ''I marvel that a Jewish theater in a 'Jewish ' organization could present a play in which a Nazi soldier is the hero and a sympathetic hero at that....You need basic courses in the Holocaust.''

Elephants, staged in December 1981, also brought in mixed messages: ''Thank you for the wonderful play and for its marvelous performances. In appreciation we enclose a year-end gift to your theater,'' wrote one couple. But another man wrote, ''It brings in vicious acrimonious relations between father and son, the dragging in of an ugly bag woman to abet a plan to raise money by dope peddling. I left after the first act, a bad taste in my mouth.''

A play like Pinter's *The Homecoming*, which ran in February 1984, brought more positive than negative mail: ''It was very moving, the acting superb and it was the most professional of all the productions we have seen at the JRT....unforgettable evening,'' and ''acting absolutely brilliant...I hope you get the great reviews you all deserve.'' But, on the other hand: ''a grievous, shameful error of judgement. Was this a play relating to the Jewish experience? By no stretch of the imagination!''

The letters revealed more about the writers than the plays they were assessing. Many of the writers criticized the JRT when it presented Jews in a bad light, as they saw it, regardless of the quality of the plays or performances. They were particularly touchy about such subjects as the Holocaust or intermarriage or free-wheeling, sexually liberated contemporary young Jews. Clearly the favorite subject matter was Jewish life in another time and place—and a sentimentalized, glamorized version of that life, to be sure. At the same time, they expected productions to be well done, with excellent directors, actors, set designers.

In short, such theatergoers mandated professional productions combined with inoffensive subject matter. Of course there were some theatergoers who looked for material of substance and truth. The artistic director was forced to weigh diverse audience demands against the dictates of his own taste and conscience—a position that every artistic director faces. The JRT differed in that there were the added ingredients of touchiness and loyalty to the particular cultural group.

Based on the letters and the questionnaire responses, one can reach certain general conclusions about the JRT audiences. They are mostly older, married, professional, Jewish New Yorkers. In their relationship to the JRT, they are fiercely loyal, deeply involved, and often highly critical. They are mostly conservative in taste and have a strong sense of their own Jewishness, however they might define that word. They have broad cultural interests and attend many other theaters and cultural events, but when it comes to their own "Jewish theater," they define the appropriate fare narrowly.

---

[1]The JRT officials have asked me not to identify the writers of these letters in any way. I have therefore not used footnotes to indicate the specific source of the letters. All are taken from the JRT correspondence files.

[2]Ran Avni, letter to a subscriber, 16 April 1984.

CHAPTER

7

CONCLUSION

The main focus of this dissertation was to chronicle the initial ten-year period of the Jewish Repertory Theatre, with special attention to the methods and significant contributions of the founder and artistic director, Ran Avni.

The secondary purposes are: first, to call attention to the growing significance of Jewish theater in America (as exemplified by the Jewish Repertory Theatre) and, second, to point out the distinctions, as well as similarities, between this movement and the Yiddish theater of the past.

Certain questions were posed: First, what is Jewish theater? The old Yiddish theater had no difficulty with that question, because the language itself was the determining factor. People who spoke Yiddish came to see plays performed in Yiddish. But the contemporary theaters which call themselves Jewish use a language that in no way distinguishes them from mainstream theater; thus they must define themselves in different terms. I have found, in questioning artistic directors of many American Jewish theaters (such as Debra Olchick of the Berkely Jewish Theater and Stanley Brechner of the American Jewish Theater), that there is no clearcut answer to the question— or rather there are as many answers as there are respondents. American Jews themselves are questioning their identity, seeking to determine whether there is anything in their religion or culture or values which sets them apart from their fellow Americans. Therefore, it is no surprise that the Jewish theater, a reflection of its constituency, should struggle with the same question.

The Jewish Repertory Theatre itself responds to the question in broad terms, defining Jewish theater, specifically its own theater, as one that deals with the "Jewish experience," both current and past experience. As Ran Avni views it, the question must be constantly explored and reexamined, and is, in fact, the very reason for the theater's existence.

Another question was asked: How is the new Jewish theater different from the old Yiddish theater? The chief differences are that each relates to the special audiences of its own time. The Yiddish theater met the needs of an immigrant population, hungry for escapist entertainment, but entertainment that gave its audiences, who lived within an alien culture, a sense of unity and identification. The current theater caters to a more educated audience (see Chapter 6 of this study), one which demands far more contemporary fare. At the same time, current JRT audiences expect the productions to have Jewish significance—either to hark back to their heritage or to concern themselves with current issues. Otherwise, the JRT productions would be no different from the myriad of other theatrical offerings in New York City.

Despite these differences, American Jewish theater owes a profound debt to Yiddish theater, as well as other earlier forms of Jewish theater. Therefore, the opening chapter provided a brief overview of early Jewish history, explaining Judaism's injunctions against theater, while, at the same time, acknowledging its attraction. It traced the Jews' wanderings into Europe, where the annual holiday plays, the *Purimshpil*, kept a limited kind of theater alive. Not unil the nineteenth century in Russia, during a relatively emancipated era for the Jews, did the Golden Age of Yiddish theater emerge. That theater was brought to the United States with the large wave of Jewish immigration. The theater flourished as long as the Yiddish language itself continued to be the common speech of Jews, roughly through the 1920s. As Jews moved into the mainstream, so did their theater interests, with Jews contributing to the growth of Broadway and Hollywood rather than to ethnic theater. Not until the late 1960s and early 1970s, a time of social revolution and tolerance for diversity, would ethnic theater come into its own and would the stage be set once more for Jewish theater.

The second chapter of this study reported on the early years of Ran Avni, the founder of the JRT. In 1969 Avni came to this country to study theater and stayed on to launch a shoestring Jewish theater with fellow Israeli Avner Regev. In early 1975, when the theater was still more concept than reality, Don Geller, director of the Emanu-El Midtown YM-YWHA in New York City, gave the theater a home. But the Y had no previous experience with theater, and the staff tended to treat it in cavalier fashion, hardly taking it seriously. It was one more Y activity, and a nuisance activity at that. Avni, however, persisted doggedly, overcoming the resistance of a reluctant staff, turning an upstairs dance studio into a real theater.

The third chapter chronicled the JRT from its first four-play season (1975-1976) through to the 1980s. The early period shows a ragged group (mostly students from the Herbert Berghof Studio) performing before a handful of friends and relatives in a low-ceilinged room where audiences in the rear rows struck their heads when they stood up. Props and sets were makeshift, with materials scavenged from the streets and from friends' apartments. But several HB students and faculty would become the mainstay of the JRT: Lynn Polan, Michael Mantel, Alice Spivak, Don Marlette among them. Jewish performers who worked at the theater had a sense of "homecoming," they said, finding a certain comfort in the Jewish atmosphere.

In April 1977, Edward Cohen came to the JRT with his own play, *Cakes with the Wine*. The play was never performed because of a lockout of Y workers, but Cohen went on to become an integral, significant part of the operation.

In the 1977-1978 season Avni was paid for the first time (an annual salary of $10,000), Betsy Imershein joined the staff, and Alfred Plant formed a JRT board of directors. The May 1978 production of *I Am a Camera* brought the *New York Times* critic to the JRT for the first time. Gradually, the JRT was building its audience, depending primarily on people in the immediate neighborhood, who found the Jewish themes heart-warming and the theater's location convenient.

The 1978-1979 season saw Immershein become managing director, and subscriptions were launched, initially bringing in 200 subscribers. Cohen, who had been evaluating new scripts and advising young playwrights, initiated his Writer's Lab, which staged readings of new works.

In 1979-1980, the company moved from Equity showcase status (in which no one was paid) to Equity's Non-Profit Theater Code, Tier One. Actors, directors, and stage managers were paid on a per show basis. And in March 1980, the company's *Green Fields*, directed by Lynn Polan, brought a strong review from the *New York Times*. With the positive reactions of major papers, the JRT began to build a broader-based audience, reaching people throughout the city and in the suburbs.

Arthur Miller became involved with the theater in 1980-1981, when his *Incident at Vichy* was staged in June. Miller claimed it was the best production of his play he had seen, a view echoed by the critics and audiences, and Avni saw it as a highlight of his directing career.

In 1981-1982, the company's *Awake and Sing!* featured the successful team of Polan-Mantel and set designer Jeffrey Schneider, again evoking rave reviews from the *New York Times* and other newspapers. In June of that season the musical *Vagabond Stars* launched the new team of Nahma Sandrow-Raphael Crystal and was so successful that Avni extended the run into the summer. Thus the theater began a practice of ending each season with a musical.

In 1982-1983 Edward Cohen received a National Endowment for the Arts grant, enabling him to give more time to the JRT and to launch a playwrights-in-residence program. He brought together seven of his most promising young playwrights, working with them closely on scripts, staged readings, and, ultimately, full productions.

In 1983-1984, the JRT went to an Equity mini-contract, with actors paid on a weekly basis, including rehearsal time. It was the year of *Kuni-Leml*, a musical that ultimately became a legend, moving from the JRT to the uptown Broadway area and finally across the country. *Kuni-Leml* featured he Sandrow-Crystal team, with Richard Engquist as lyricist. It was based on an old Yiddish play, and the writers combined the old story with delightful new songs that retained the old feeling. *Kuni-Leml* was the JRT's biggest financial, as well as popular, success, and firmly established the company as a first-rate theater.

The following season, subscriptions, which had been building slowly, jumped from 900 to 1500, mostly as a response to *Kuni-Leml*. The season opened with a premiere of a new Isaac Bashevis Singer play, which was not a success, although the connection to Singer lent prestige to the theater. The hit of the season in April 1985 was *Crossing Delancey*, a delightful contemporary comedy that had its roots solidly planted in the past (the Jewish immigrant experience).

Although not all performances over the ten years were successes, the seasons were peppered with enough highlights to enable the JRT to develop a solid reputation. Gradually, more and more established writers, directors, actors (such as Arthur Miller, Isaac Singer, Austin Pendleton, Len Cariou) were drawn to the JRT, willing to settle for token pay because of its reputation and the opportunity to work on Jewish plays. And former students Lynn Polan, Michael Mantel and Jeffrey Schneider, who went on to be professionals, who had their start at the JRT, returned again and again to the theater.

What accounts for the JRT's ability to survive, grow and gain recognition? Like so many of today's regional theaters, as well as notable theaters of the past, the key ingredient is the artistic director. The artistic director is pivotal. Ultimately, it is his vision, his charisma, his commitment, his tenacity, his particular stamp on a theater, that determines its success or failure.

Ran Avni has those ingredients in generous amounts. Though he insists he is a pragmatist, not an intellectual or visionary, the fact is that he has had a vision of the company he wanted to create. And he held on to that vision, even while he lived on unemployment checks and performed the menial as well as artistic tasks that had to be done. He had a faith in his theater in its darkest hours—even when he had to battle with drunken maintenance men or plead for money for props or replace an actor at the last minute or face Equity punishment for extending a show.

On the practical side, Avni has an uncanny sense of what works on stage and what his audiences will accept, although he is open to the exploration of all kinds of plays, drawn from many different periods in Jewish history. He has been persuaded at times to ignore that instinct, at which point he has paid the price in audience disapproval.

Looking back at the JRT's first ten years, I see much that has worked well, but also much that could be changed. The first point in question is whether the JRT should have stayed on at the Y or found a home of its own. There were, to begin, the limitations imposed by the building rules. For example, the Y was closed Friday evenings and Saturdays because of the Sabbath, making it difficult to rehearse Saturdays. Also, the JRT lost Friday nights for performances, an important night for theatergoers. Secondly, theatergoers could not walk in off the street, to a street-level theater; they had to take an elevator to the second floor. There was, in fact, no evidence from the outside that a theater existed at all. Lastly, there were the problems Avni had with the Y staff itself in terms of finances and suportive services, because of staff members' indifference and the demands of other Y activities.

Others, particularly Betsy Imershein as managing director, pointed out these drawbacks to Avni, but he stubbornly chose to remain. He argued that the main advantage was financial.

Avni has been right. When all was said and done, the Y spelled security, providing theater space as well as ancillary services. Avni was well aware of the high mortality rate for small off-off-Broadway houses. If the JRT had to meet its own expenses by raising ticket prices, Avni was convinced he would surely lose his audience. One attractive feature of the JRT had always been the price of its tickets. Furthermore, the Y gives the JRT an identity as a Jewish theater by virtue of its very location and also reaches people who are there for other activities. Moreover, the JRT is following a pattern that has proved to be workable across the country. Most of the other American-Jewish theaters, amateur or professional, are located at Jewish YMHAs or community centers.

In all, I think the JRT has been wise to remain although much could and should be done to improve the premises. The theater itself is still makeshift, with a lighting booth that operates out of a barely concealed former kitchen. There are no wings or backstage area, dressing rooms are non-existent, and audiences continue to sit on rickety chairs. Worst of all, the lobby is a narrow hallway, and bathroom facilities are crumbling and poorly tended.

The new, upcoming theater, to be built as soon as two million dollars are raised, will, it is hoped, correct these problems. Yet one hopes that a certain magic that adheres to the little theater (former dance classroom) will not be lost.

The JRT has done well in providing opportunity, not only for the actors and directors, but also for the playwrights. Edward Cohen's Playwrights-in-Residence program offered a secure, ongoing haven that writers seldom enjoy in the fiercely competitive theater world. Whether or not a particular play is right for the JRT, Cohen continues to work with the writer.

As to choice of plays, the JRT, as the pioneer in the current Jewish theater movement, has forged into new territory. Often other theaters have followed the JRT's lead, several years later producing a play that first made its appearance at the JRT.

Avni discovered English translations of little-known Yiddish and Hebrew plays, staging them at the JRT. Both *God of Vengeance* and *Green Fields*, translated from the Yiddish by Queens College professor Joseph Landis, were fresh experiences for American audiences. And the musicals *Pearls* and *Kuni-Leml* were based on old Yiddish plays by Jacob Gordin and Avrom Goldfadn respectively, but proved to be meaningful to contemporary audiences.

Avni has revived old favorties, such as *Awake and Sing!* by Clifford Odets and Arthur Miller's *Incident at Vichy*, presenting them in fresh new formats that were often superior to the original stagings. And the company has reexplored old classics, looking for the significance to Jews in such works as Shakespeare's *Merchant of Venice* and Chekhov's *Ivanov*. Moreover, he has provided a forum for the contemporary young American Jewish writers. Not only the works of the playwrights in residence, but many other scripts that crossed Edward Cohen's desk were given a reading that sometimes led to a full production.

Not all the plays produced at the JRT, however, had a clear-cut connection to the "Jewish experience." I question the choice of

Clifford Odets's *Rocket to the Moon* or Harold Pinter's work. Granted the writers are Jewish, and, as such, must be influenced by their backgrounds. But one must search (and a number of critics have done so) to identify *The Homecoming* and *The Birthday Party* with the Jewish experience.

Other questionable choices included several plays about German families in the post-Nazi period—*Jonah, Anna Kleiber*, and *The Condemned of Altona*. I concede that, while the plays are not clearly relevant, the mentality of post-Nazi Germans would interest Jewish audiences.

Other choices like Thornton Wilder's *The Matchmaker* and Ronald Ribman's *Cold Storage* have no reason whatsoever to be included, since neither includes Jewish characters (as far as one knows) or Jewish themes. But given a track record of some sixty Jewish-type plays over the years, the company can be forgiven two such errors.

In all, the JRT has presented a rich, diverse program that has looked at Jews in many times and places. Its choices have been basically conservative in format and subject matter, but that is what suits the JRT audiences. That is what works and keeps the audiences coming back. Several original works, comic in form but serious in themes, that dwelt on sometimes sordid but highly relevant, contemporary subjects, were rejected by the conservative JRT audiences.

I think the JRT should make a strong effort to bring young, adventurous theatergoers into the theater. Of course, Avni does not want to lose his loyal audience, but there is also a place and a need for more daring, serious work that speaks directly to our time. Cohen took a step in this direction by offering a month-long program in March 1987 called "Our Own Family," in which new short works by the playwrights in residence were presented.

Having established itself as a spiritual force in the new American-Jewish theater movement, the JRT should assume a more active leadership role, perhaps launching an organization for the growing Jewish theater community. Networking and sharing of ideas and problems could be invaluable.

Meanwhile, with some thirty English-speaking Jewish companies scattered across the country—and at least seven of them professional—the movement has indeed become a reality. New professional theaters have sprung up recently in Miami and Chica-

go, and theaters in New York, San Francisco, and Berkeley continue
to thrive.

The Jewish Repertory Theatre has never aspired to leadership, but
nonetheless it has become an important institution, both in terms of
its own accomplishments and in its role as a model for the entire
American Jewish theater movement.

APPENDIX A
JEWISH REPERTORY THEATRE PROGRAMS

1974-1975
GOD OF VENGEANCE   October 1974
LADY OF THE CASTLE   April 1975

1975-1976
A NIGHT IN MAY   September 1975
RELATIVES and   November 1975
   THE CLOSING OF MENDEL'S CAFE
ANDORRA   February 1976
EAST SIDE JUSTICE   June 1976

1976-1977
MIDDLE OF THE NIGHT   September 1976
JONAH   October 1976
CAFE CROWN   December 1976
THE CONDEMNED OF ALTONA   February 1977
CAKES WITH THE WINE   April 1977 (cancelled)
IVANOV   June 1977

1977-1978
THE COLD WIND AND THE WARM   October 1977
DANCING IN NEW YORK CITY   December 1977
THE MERCHANT OF VENICE   February 1977
ANNA KLEIBER   March 1978
I AM A CAMERA   May 1978
I AM A ZOO   June 1978

1978-1979
TRIPTYCH and SAMMI   October 1978
THE HALLOWEEN BANDIT   December 1978
UNLIKELY HEROES   January 1979
LOYALTIES   March 1979
THE GENTLE PEOPLE   May 1979
ROCKET TO THE MOON   June 1979

1979-1980
LILIOM   October 1979
BENYA THE KING   December 1979
THE MATCHMAKER   January 1980
GREEN FIELDS   March 1980
COME BLOW YOUR HORN   April 1980
36 (extended into summer)   June 1980

APPENDIX A
JEWISH REPERTORY THEATRE PROGRAMS
(continued)

1980-1981
ME AND MOLLY   October 1980
SUCCESS STORY   December 1980
THE BIRTHDAY PARTY   January 1981
MARYA   March 1981
INCIDENT AT VICHY   May 1981
   (brought back September 1981)

1981-1982
AWAKE AND SING!   October 1981
ELEPHANTS   December 1981
DELMORE   February 1982
PATAGLEIZE   April 1982
VAGABOND STARS   June 1982
   (summer extension)

1982-1983
AFTER THE FALL   October 1982
FRIENDS TOO NUMEROUS TO MENTION   December 1982
IVANOV   February 1983
TAKING STEAM   April 1983
MY HEART IS IN THE EAST   June 1983
   (summer extension)

1983-1984
UP FROM PARADISE   October 1983
GIFTED CHILDREN   December 1983
THE HOMECOMING   February 1984
ESCAPE FROM RIVERDALE   April 1984
KUNI-LEML   June 1984
   (summer extension)

1984-1985
SHLEMIEL THE FIRST   October 1984
COLD STORAGE   December 1984
CITY BOY   February 1985
CROSSING DELANCEY   May 1985
PEARLS   July 1985

APPENDIX B
AUDIENCE SURVEY

As my Ph.D. disseration, I am writing a ten-year history of the Jewish Repertory Theatre. You, the JRT audience, are a crucial part of that history. Your
profile, your interests and concerns, will enrich the history and will also help
the JRT in future program planning. Therefore, would you please complete this
questionnaire, but omitting whatever you wish. We appreciate your cooperation.

Your relation to the JRT

Are you a subscriber? _____ For how long? _____

Why did you subscribe? _____

Do you attend all productions? _____ Why or why not?

_____

If not a subscriber, how did you hear about JRT? _____

_____

Why did you attend this performance? _____

In what way is the JRT a ''Jewish theater'' to you? _____

_____

JRT plays and productions

Your favorite JRT plays: _____

Why? _____

What productions did you like the least? _____

Why? _____

Rank your preference, from #1 (first choice) to #6:

musicals _____ comedies _____ serious plays _____

classics _____ new works _____ other _____

What other plays would you like to see at the JRT?

_____

Are you aware of the JRT's Writers' Lab? _____

Children's Theater? _____

Do you attend staged readings at the JRT? _____

What changes would you like to see at the JRT? _____

_____

What so you think of the theater space itself—and its location at the

Midtown Y? _____

_____

APPENDIX B
AUDIENCE SURVEY
(Continued)

Your general interest in theater and the arts

Do you support other arts? _____ Which? _____
_____

Do you subscribe to or attend other theaters? _____
   Which? _____
What other plays have you seen recently? _____
_____

Do you attend occasionally or subscribe to the American
   Jewish Theater at the 92nd Street Y? _____
If so, what differences do you see between the AJT and the JRT?
_____

Personal data

Name (optional) _____
Address (optional) _____
Age _____ Sex _____ Marital Status _____
Occupation _____
Education (highest degree) _____
Dwelling (house or apartment, owned or rented) _____
Income: under $15,000 _____ $15,000 to $34,999 _____
   $35,000 to $59,999 _____ $60,000 to $79,999 _____
   $80,000 and over   _____
Religion _____ If Jewish, are you a
   practicing Jew? _____ Conservative _____ Orthodox _____
   Reform _____ Other _____
   Temple/Synagogue you attend _____

PLEASE USE SPACE ON BACK OF PAGES FOR FURTHER
COMMENTS. LEAVE QUESTIONNAIRE IN LOBBY OR MAIL TO:
Irene Backalenick, 373 Greens Farms Road, Westport, Connecticut 06880.

BOOKS

EARLY HEBREW AND LADINO THEATER
Gaster, Theodor H. *Thespis: Ritual, Myth and Drama in the Ancient Near East,* second revised ed. New York: Gordian Press, 1975.

ENCYCLOPEDIAS
de Haas, Jacob, ed. *Encyclopedia of Jewish Knowledge.* New York: Behrman's Jewish Book House, 1934.
Roth, Cecil, ed. *Standard Jewish Encyclopedia,* new revised ed. Garden City: Doubleday and Co., 1962.

ETHNIC AMERICA
Johnson, Harry. *Ethnic American Minorities.* New York: Allwyn Press, 1976.
Keyes, Charles F., ed. *Ethnic Change.* (Publications on Ethnicity and Nationality of the School of International Studies.) Seattle: University of Washington Press, 1981.
McDonagh, Edward C. and Richards, Eugene S. *Ethnic Relations in the United States.* Westport, Ct.: Greenwood Press, 1972.
Petersen, William and Novak, Michael. *Concepts of Ethnicity.* Cambridge, Mass.: Harvard University Press, 1982.
Stack, John, ed. *Ethnic Identities in a Transactional World.* Westport, Ct.: Greenwood Press, 1981.

ETHNIC THEATER
Seller, Maxine S., ed. *Ethnic Theater in the United States.* Westport, Ct.: Greenwood Press, 1983.

GENERAL
Introduction to Treasury of Yiddish Literature. New York: Meridian Books, 1958.

JEWISH HISTORY
Finkelstein, Louis. *The Jews: Their History, Culture and Religion,* third ed. New York: Harper and Row, 1960.
Handlin, Oscar. *Adventures in Freedom, 300 Years of Jewish Life in America.* Port Washington, N.Y.: Kennikat Press, 1971.
Howe, Irving. *World of our Fathers.* New York: Harcourt, Brace, Jovanovich, 1976.
Howe, Irving, and Libo, Kenneth. *How We Lived—A Documentary History of Immigrant Jews in America, 1880-1930.* New York: Richard March Publishers, 1979.
Joseph, Samuel. *Jewish Immigration to the United States from 1881 to 1910.* New York: Arno Press, 1969.
Margolis, Max, and Marx, Alexander. *History of the Jewish People.* Philadelphia: Jewish Publication Society of America, 1941.

THE IMAGE OF THE JEW IN DRAMA AND LITERATURE

Cohen, Edward, ed. *Plays of Jewish Interest*. New York: Jewish Theater Association, 1983.

Harap, Louis. *The Image of the Jew in American Literature*. Philadelphia: Jewish Publication Society of America, 1978.

Landa, Myer Jack. *The Jew in Drama*. Port Washington, N.Y.: Kennikat Press, 1968.

Rosenberg, Edgar. *From Shylock to Svengali*. Palo Alto: Stanford University Press, 1960.

YIDDISH THEATER

Cohen, Sarah B. *From Hester Street to Hollywood—The Jewish-American Stage and Screen*. Bloomington, Ind.: Indiana University Press, 1983.

Lifson, David. *Yiddish Theatre in America*. New York: T. Yoseloff, 1965.

Rosenfeld, Lulla. *Bright Star of Exile*. New York: Thomas Y. Crowell Company, 1977.

Sandrow, Nahma. *Vagabond Stars*. New York: Harper and Row, 1977.

CLIPPINGS

Newspaper and magazine articles and theater reviews, JRT documents and correspondence, 1974-1985, on file at the Emanu-El Midtown YM-YWHA, New York City.

PERSONAL INTERVIEWS

Avni, Ran. New York City. 5 February 1985.
                              6 June 1985.
                              16 July 1985.
                              19 July 1985.
                              22 July 1985.
                              14 September 1985.
                              4 December 1985.
                              17 December 1985.
                              28 July 1986.

Cohen, Edward. New York City. 6 December 1984.
                              17 February 1986.

Crystal, Raphael, New York City. 14 March 1986.

Ellentuck, Dan. New York City. 16 November 1984.

Geller, Don. New York City. 28 March 1985.
                              4 December 1985.
                              16 September 1986.

Imershein, Betsy. New York City. 13 June 1985.

Mantel, Michael Albert. New York City. 28 May 1985.

PERSONAL INTERVIEWS (continued)

Margulies, Donald. New Haven, Conn. 5 October 1984.
McKay, Anthony. Westport, Conn. 30 December 1985.
Plant, Alfred. New York City. 18 October 1984.
Polan, Lynn. New York City. 5 April 1985.
Rosenberg, David. New York City. 22 July 1985.
Sandler, Susan. New York City. 19 November 1984.
Sandrow, Nahma. New York City. 13 November 1984.
Schlamme, Martha. New York City. 20 February 1985.
Schnabel, Stefan. Rowayton, Conn. 15 October 1985.
Schneider, Jeffrey. New York City. 10 June 1985.
Schotter, Richard. New York City. 8 November 1984.
Smith, Ray. New York City. 31 May 1985.
Spergel, Mark. New York City. 29 May 1985.
Spivak, Alice. New York City. 31 May 1985.
Taav, Michael, New York City. 6 November 1984.
Wollner, Don. New York City. 19 October 1984.

PERSONAL INTERVIEWS FOR BACKGROUND MATERIAL

Stanley Brechner, Frances Brumlik, Debra Crane, Meyer Gutwillig, Tamar Hirschberg, Jackie Jacob, Cynthia Kolker, Deborah Olchick, Michael Price, Dorothy Silver, Tamir.